SACRAMENTO

HEART OF THE GOLDEN STATE

SACRAMENTO

HEART OF THE GOLDEN STATE

JOSEPH A. McGOWAN & TERRY R. WILLIS

Pictorial Research by Lucinda Woodward
"Partners in Progress" by Terry R. Willis

Produced in Cooperation with the
Sacramento County Historical Society

Windsor Publications, Inc.
Woodland Hills, California

Windsor Publications, Inc.
History Books Division
Publisher: John M. Phillips
Editorial Director: Lissa Sanders
Production Supervisor: Katherine Cooper
Senior Picture Editor: Teri Davis Greenberg
Senior Corporate History Editor: Karen Story
Marketing Director: Ellen Kettenbeil
Production Manager: James Burke
Design Director: Alexander D'Anca
Art Production Manager: Dee Cooper
Typesetting Manager: E. Beryl Myers

Windsor Publications' Staff for
Sacramento: Heart of the Golden State
Editor: Pamela Taylor
Text Editor: Todd Ackerman
Picture Editor: Kevin Cavanaugh
Corporate History Editor: Karen Story
Sales Manager: Steve Allison
Sales Representative: Robert Fay
Editorial Assistants: Susan Block, Patricia Dailey, Phyllis
    Gray, Judy Hunter
Compositors: Shannon Mellies, Barbara Neiman
Proofreaders: Doris R. Malkin, Ruth H. Hoover
Production Artists: Constance Blaisdell, Ellen Hazeltine,
    Colleen Maggart

Designer: Melinda Wade

Previous facing page: Courtesy,
Sacramento Bee Collection,
Sacramento Museum and History
Division

Library of Congress Cataloging in Publication Data
McGowan, Joseph A.
    Sacramento, heart of the Golden State.

    "Produced in cooperation with Sacramento County
Historical Society."
    Bibliography: p. 155
    Includes index.
    1. Sacramento (Calif.)—History. 2. Sacramento
(Calif.)—Description. 3. Sacramento (Calif.)—
Industries. I. Willis, Terry R., 1939-
II. Sacramento County Historical Society. III. Title.
F869.S12M38   1983   979.4'54   83-4088
ISBN 0-89781-066-X

TABLE OF CONTENTS

PREFACE

There are many kinds of history, ranging from the encyclopedic, where facts tend to submerge interpretation, to interpretative histories where the reverse is true. The authors have tried to steer a path between these two extremes. Our objective has been to tell the Sacramento story, how the city was born, and how it grew to its present metropolitan status. Such an approach has necessarily been interpretative, which required us to exclude much factual material and to give only a line or two to subjects which themselves could occupy dozens of pages.

In the process of doing the research we have acquired an enormous respect for the valley's aggressive and persevering pioneers, and the pioneering spirit which still exists today. We only wish we had time and space to share more of the adventure, the follies, the triumphs, and the controversies which were a part of the building of the city. In tracing the main develop-

ments which made the metropolitan area what it is today, we could only hint at the opposition, the politicking, the—well, let's put it bluntly—the *bickering* which accompanied every step forward. The pioneers not only contended with the forces of nature, but also with the perversities of human nature. The result, for all of its imperfections, is a remarkable creation, still growing and evolving. Despite differences of opinion or means, the prevailing ethic is still one of social responsibility and civic betterment.

We have thoroughly enjoyed the privilege of tracing the history of the city and county of Sacramento. We hope that long-time residents will recognize the story we tell and that more recent arrivals will sense a feeling for the area and thereby understand their heritage.

Joseph A. McGowan
Terry R. Willis

One of Sacramento's first suburbs was Oak Park, founded in 1889. Sacramento's streetcar lines reached the city in 1904, and Oak Park was annexed by the capital in 1911. Sacramento's city assessment rolls designated Oak Park and East Sacramento as ''annexed territories.'' Courtesy, California State Library Collection, SMHD

ACKNOWLEDGMENTS

In telling the story of Sacramento we have had the generous assistance of many people in the community. We would like to take this opportunity to mention a few, in particular, who have contributed above and beyond the call of duty.

First, a special thank you to Barry Cassidy, former president of the Sacramento County Historical Society, who had faith in the project from the beginning; and to Douglas W. Griffith, president of Golden State Business Systems, for the generous use of office space and equipment, plus support and encouragement.

For assistance in the photographic research we are indebted to photo-historian Nikki Pahl, who copied most of the images in this book with an eye to both the aesthetic effect and the historical significance. The Sacramento History Center graciously opened up its extensive photographic archives. Director James E. Henley, Sherry Hatch, Steve Helmich, and the entire staff were most helpful. Walter P. Gray, III, archivist at the California State Railroad Museum, provided guidance through the museum's vast collection of railroad photographs. The *Elk Grove Citizen* shared its news photos of recent historical celebrations. Several individuals opened their personal collections of Sacramento photographs and ephemera, including Donald Napoli, Henry and Sally Taketa, and Norman L. Wilson. Norm deserves a special thank you in particular for his expertise in the subject areas of Native Americans and 19th century Sacramento. George Stammerjohan's publicity photos early in the project got us off to a good start.

A number of people helped us locate documents and shared their expertise on various aspects of modern-day Sacramento. Among them were Walter Christensen, Carol Guilbault, Thomas Hammer, Eugene Itogawa, Bob Krieger, John Morgan, Joseph Samora, Douglas Willis, and the staff in the City Engineer's office. In addition, we are the beneficiaries of much independent, original research in the form of term papers and theses by students of history at California State University, Sacramento.

The city and county are fortunate in having excellent research facilities for local history. We have spent many pleasant and rewarding hours in the California Room of the California State Library, the University Library on the campus in Sacramento, the Sacramento City College Library, and the various branches of the Sacramento City-County Library.

Because of our special interest in historic preservation, we would like to pay tribute at this time to a few of Sacramento's farsighted and dedicated public servants for their efforts long before preservation became a popular cause. Playing key roles in the early development of Old Sacramento were the late Senator Earl Desmond, the late Assemblyman Edwin Z'berg; and Frank Durkee, who was chairman of the Redevelopment Commission for many years. Senator Albert Rodda, along with members of the Pacific Chapter of the Railway and Locomotive Historical Society, secured state support for the construction of the new Railroad Museum. Edgar Sayre, former city councilman, and the late V. Aubrey Neasham, historian, were instrumental in the establishment of the Sacramento History Center.

Last but not least, we would like to express our profound appreciation to the Sacramento County Historical Society for co-sponsoring this book, to each of the Sacramento area businesses participating in the Partners in Progress section, and to our publishers, Windsor Publication, Inc., for making it possible.

Joseph A. McGowan
Terry R. Willis
Lucinda M. Woodward
Sacramento, California

Chapter 1

THE SUTTER YEARS
1839-1849

One man's 10-year venture in the wilderness turned out to be the first stage in the rise of a lively, cosmopolitan, commercial, and political center—Sacramento. The discovery of gold which was to change the course of history for California and the nation originated directly through Sutter's activities in building up his settlement—and ironically, caused the settlement's downfall.

In 1839 a Swiss adventurer carrying Mexican papers landed on the bank of the American River, in a wilderness territory inhabited by Indians. Ten years later the primitive trading post he built there gave birth to Sacramento, capital city of California.

The adventurer, John Augustus Sutter, had visited several Mexican military outposts in Alta California, then a province of the Mexican government, but turned down invitations by Mexican officials to settle near any of them.

"I had noticed very well," he later explained, "that one's hat had to be taken off before the military guard, the flag staff, and the church. I preferred a country where I could keep my hat on. I wanted to be my own master."

Since leaving his wife and children in Switzerland in 1834 (it is believed he came to the United States to escape imprisonment for debt) Sutter had spent five years making his way across the American continent in company with trappers, traders, and soldiers. Always an admirer of military protocol, he dined with officers and heads of state, and, in the course of his travels, assigned himself the rank of captain and described himself as a former officer in the Swiss army. While in the Midwest, he joined a group of trappers who told him about the lush vegetation and plentiful game in the Sacramento Valley in the interior region of Alta California.

He traveled with them to their summer rendezvous in Wyoming, where trappers and Indians gathered to barter, trade, drink, gamble, and celebrate. There he bought an Indian boy who spoke English, Spanish, and several Indian dialects to act as guide.

In company with a group of trappers, missionaries, and Indians, Sutter headed, in a circuitous route, for Alta California. He traveled by horse and mule to Fort Vancouver, a Hudson's Bay Company trading post on the Columbia River in Oregon territory; by sailing ship to the Sandwich Isles (now Hawaii) where he stayed for five months; by another sailing ship to Sitka, Alaska, where he delivered a cargo of goods to the Russian settlement; and, finally, by sailing ship down the coast to his original destination, California. He stopped briefly at Yerba Buena (a small military outpost which changed its name in 1847 to San Francisco), then continued south to the Mexican provincial capital at Monterey.

The Mexican governor, Juan Bautista Alvarado, urged Sutter to find a site to his liking and return in a year's time to receive Mexican citizenship and a grant of land. After Sutter sailed back to Yerba Buena, he visited a few outposts of civilization nearby. There he payed his respects to the Mexican military commandant, General Mariano Vallejo, who was in charge of a garrison of about 50 men at Sonoma, and the Russian commandant, Alexander Rotchev, at the Fort Ross settlement on the coast about 85 miles to the north of San Francisco Bay.

Back in Yerba Buena Sutter chartered two schooners, the *Isabella* and the *Nicholas*, and bought a small boat with four oars and a sail to serve as a scout ship. With the boats in readiness, he rounded up the members of his expedition. Including the two ships' captains and crews, the party consisted of about two dozen men, two women, and one large bulldog. Leaving Yerba Buena early in August 1839, the party spent several days exploring the easterly reaches of the San Francisco Bay. At length they found the mouth of the Sacramento River.

As they rowed and sailed up the river, they saw bunches of white feathers which the Miwok Indians had tied to the overhanging branches of the trees as offerings to the spirits. Indians had lived in the area for over 2,000 years, fishing, hunting, and gathering acorns. Their homes of mud and tule

Facing page: Swiss adventurer John Sutter, Sr., founded the 48,000 acre rancho of New Helvetia in 1839. Sutter built his empire by acquiring Mexican land grants and using political alliances and Indian labor. Courtesy, California State Library

California's Central Valley was densely occupied by the Nisenan, Patwin, and Miwok Indians. Villages lined the American and Sacramento rivers. In the 1840s and 1850s immigrant settlements displaced these Indian villages, many of which had been continuously occupied for over 2,000 years. Courtesy, Norman L. Wilson

reeds were clustered in villages, some containing as many as several hundred people.

When Sutter reached a spot about 12 miles below the junction of the American River, he saw about 200 Indians in red, yellow, and black ceremonial paint gathered in a clearing, waiting and watching. He jumped ashore and shouted what he thought was the Spanish greeting, "Adios, amigos!"

Two mission-educated Indians stepped forward and answered in Spanish. After the captain had persuaded them his intentions were friendly, they relayed the message to their companions, then joined the expedition as guides. The party explored upriver to the Feather River, passing many villages of the Nisenan Indians—whose territory extended generally north of the Cosumnes River—along the way. Then Sutter and company floated back down to the junction of the American River and sailed up the American a little more than two miles, where they tied their boats to trees on the south bank. (The course of the river was changed in 1868 to prevent floods, and the present-day location of the landing spot is approximately 29th and B streets.)

The date recorded in Sutter's diary was August 12, 1839. The crew unloaded the tents, supplies, and three brass cannons from the schooners. Since the men were complaining about the heat and mosquitoes, Sutter called all hands together and told them that anyone who wanted to leave could go back to Yerba Buena on the schooners the next morning. Six of them chose to return.

As the schooners prepared to depart, hundreds of Indians gathered to watch. By way of a proper military farewell, Sutter's men loaded the cannons and fired a nine-gun salute. The men on board the boats returned the salute with a hearty "hip-hip-hooray!" At the sudden, loud noise, wild animals panicked. William Davis, captain of the *Isabella*, described the scene:

> *A large number of deer, elk, and other animals of the plains were startled, running to and fro, while from the interior of the adjacent woods the howls of wolves and coyotes filled the air, and immense flocks of water fowl flew wildly about the camp.*

The schooners slipped out of sight and an international group of settlers remained for Sutter's new establishment. Ten Kanakas—eight men and two women—had accompanied him (and the bulldog) from the Sandwich Isles.

His Indian guide, as well as three Europeans—a German, a Belgian, and an Irishman—had also cast their lots with the man who wanted to be his own master.

Walking inland a short distance south of the landing spot, Sutter found a low rise in the otherwise level terrain. There he set up camp and gave it the name New Helvetia (New Switzerland) after his homeland. The Kanakas built grass houses with tule roofs. Indians made adobe bricks for the captain's personal quarters and cleared a two-mile path to a landing site on the Sacramento River (now the Old Sacramento waterfront), which was given the Spanish name *embarcadero* (landing).

Sutter bought livestock and supplies on credit from a neighbor, Ygnacio Martinez, owner of the Rancho Pinole on Suisun Bay near the Carquinez Straits, about 50 miles from Sutter's encampment.

Late one night while most of the men had gone to bring back livestock from the Rancho Pinole, two Indians sneaked past the Kanaka sentry with knives drawn, apparently intending to kill Sutter in order to steal his goods. The bulldog attacked and held both intruders. Sutter scolded them and let them go.

That winter, from December 1839 through January 1840, heavy rains swelled the rivers and flooded the plain. Sutter's New Helvetia, like other uplands, became an island. Deer, elk, cattle, and horses huddled together on its highest ground. The heavy rain and unpredictable currents made sending the little boat to Yerba Buena for supplies impossible, and the colony subsisted on meat alone for many days. In February the water subsided and the settlers resumed the building of their civilization in the wilderness.

Sutter planned to make agriculture the economic base for his new colony. He obtained seeds and taught the Indians to break up the soil with a crude hoe, a stick with a piece of flat iron for a point—an instrument then known derisively as the California plow. When the small stand of wheat was ready for harvest, the Indians cut the stalks with hunting knives or sharp fragments of barrel hoops, or just pulled them up by the roots. To thresh the grain the men built a large enclosure of sturdy adobe walls. They threw the wheat inside, piling it a yard or two yards deep. Indian horsemen, or *vaqueros*, rounded up a band of wild mares, herded them into the wheat-filled enclosure, and whooped and yelled to stampede them about until they trampled all the grain.

In the spring of 1840, Sutter started building his fort. In August, having established a year's residence, he returned to Governor Alvarado in Monterey and secured Mexican citizenship and title to the territory of New Helvetia, a grant of about 77 square miles.

"I received at the same time a commission as representative of the government," Sutter recalled, "and was entrusted also with judicial powers. From that time on I had power of life and death both over Indians and white people in my district."

Sutter returned from Monterey with a half a dozen new recruits, one of whom, a barrelmaker, was the first black man to live in the Sacramento Valley. By this time the adobe walls of the fort were taking shape. The settlement had grown to perhaps a dozen tule huts (homes of the Kanakas and several trappers), and Sutter's three-room adobe house with a thatched tule roof. That winter the adobe house caught fire and burned, so Sutter had a new one built nearby.

The year 1841 proved eventful as Sutter hosted visitors from France, the United States, and Russia, and acquired a wealth of tools, supplies, and livestock, and, as a result, a heavy debt. Early in the year Sutter started a cattle ranch, Hock Farm, some miles up the Feather River, well above the flood plain.

International visitors arrived in the summer and fall. The French envoy M. Eugene Duflot de Mofras stayed for the month of August. Before he left, Lt. Comdr. Cadwalader Ringgold of the U.S Navy arrived at the embarcadero, having sailed up from the San Francisco Bay with a unit of Commodore Wilkes' exploring expedition. Sutter greeted their arrival—the seven officers and the 50-man crew required six whaleboats and a launch—with a cannon salute.

"They was right surprised to find me up here in this wilderness," he recalled. "It made a very good impression upon the Indians to see so many whites are coming to see me."

In September the Russian commandant, Alexander Rotchev, arrived and invited Sutter to look over the property at Fort Ross for possible purchase. Sutter agreed to buy it for $30,000, to be paid in four annual installments of wheat, peas, beans, soap, suet, tallow, and cash. Along with the land, livestock, and about 50 wooden buildings, Sutter acquired the Russian agricultural implements, tools, a distillery, old muskets, and several cannons. He also acquired a launch, which he rechristened the *Sacramento*. It became the first sailing vessel to make regular runs between the embarcadero and Yerba Buena. By water and over land, Sutter's men brought everything that could be moved back to New Helvetia, including about 2,000 head of cattle, horses, mules, and sheep.

A second party of the Wilkes expedition arrived in October from Oregon, with about 30 botanists, geologists, officers, and sailors. The United States was quite interested in the Mexican territory of California. In the fall the first wave of Eastern immigrants began to arrive. Among them was John Bidwell, a young schoolteacher from New York, who soon became Sutter's right-hand

Many immigrants in the late 1840s traveled to the northern Sacramento Valley to settle. These immigrants are shown passing the remains of an Indian dwelling. Indians were displaced from their land by the immigrants and suffered from being exposed to the settlers' diseases, especially during the malaria epidemic of 1833. Courtesy, Norman L. Wilson

man. The Captain put Bidwell in charge of the Fort Ross property for several months, then sent him to manage Hock Farm.

As New Helvetia grew, Sutter employed Indians, Californians, and immigrants in such diverse tasks as agriculture, adobe-making, carpentry, blacksmithing, barrel making, and flour milling. He built a tannery near the spot where he first landed, for he needed hides—"California bank-notes"—to trade for goods and supplies.

By 1843 the fort was nearly complete. A Swedish university student who visited it that summer described its appearance:

> It is protected by a wall ten feet high, made of adobes, or sun-dried brick, having a turret with embrasures and loop-holes for fire-arms. Twenty-four pieces of cannon, of different sizes, can be brought to defend the walls.
>
> Against the walls on the inside are erected the storehouses of the establishment; also, a distillary to make spirits from the wheat and grapes, together with shops for coopers, blacksmiths, saddlers, granaries, and huts for the laborers. At the gateway is always stationed a servant, armed as a sentinel.
>
> In the rear of the fort is a large pond, the borders of which are planted with willows and other trees. This pond furnishes water for domestic use, and for irrigating the garden.

Sutter extended a gracious welcome to the young man from Sweden and invited him to stay for breakfast. Later, the student recalled that the menu consisted of "wholesome corn-bread, eggs, ham, an excellent piece of venison, and coffee—surprising fare for the wilderness."

Another visitor, Edwin Bryant, described a typical evening meal and its setting:

> Captain Sutter's dining-room and his table furniture do not present a very luxurious appearance. The room is unfurnished, with the exception of a common deal table standing in the center, and some benches, which are substitutes for chairs.
>
> The table, when spread, presented a correspondingly primitive simplicity of aspect and of viands. The first course consisted of good soup, served to each guest, in a china bowl, with silver spoons. The bowls, after they had been used for this purpose, were taken away and cleaned by the Indian servant and were afterwards used as tumblers or goblets, from which we drank our water.
>
> The next course consisted of two dishes of meat, one roasted and one fried, and both highly seasoned with onions. Bread, cheese, butter, and melons constituted the desert.

As the fort took shape, Sutter was able to indulge his first love: military pomp and circumstance. "The Indian boys were obliged to appear every Sunday morning for drill, well washed and neatly clad," he reported in his memoirs. "Their uniform consisted of blue drill pantaloons, white cotton shirts, and red handkerchiefs tied around their heads. They were very proud of this uniform."

Sutter's personal guard consisted of a dozen men who wore uniforms of blue or green cloth with red trimmings—part of the legacy of Fort Ross. Throughout the night one of the guards stood watch by a half-hour glass.

John Bidwell served as Sutter's right-hand man during the 1840s. Following his arrival in 1841, Bidwell worked at the fort and at Hock Farm. After acquiring Rancho Chico in 1850 Bidwell participated in politics and agriculture. This portrait, by famed Civil War photographer Mathew Brady, was made in 1850. Courtesy, California State Library

Acorns were a principal food of the Central California Indians. Since acorns could be stored and used when other foods were scarce, Indians could live in permanent villages with concentrated populations. The acorns were ground, leached, made into mush, and then boiled in large baskets. The oak forests that once abounded in the area provided a large supply of acorns. Courtesy, Norman L. Wilson

Every time the sand ran out, the guard struck a bell—brought from Fort Ross—and called out, "All's well!" The same bell was rung at daybreak, summer and winter, to rouse all hands to get up and go to work.

Late in 1844 Sutter received a call for help from Manuel Micheltorena, the Mexican governor who had replaced Alvarado. Groups of restless Californians had organized an armed revolt against Micheltorena's regime and were marching on Monterey. Sutter's interest lay in the maintenance of established authority, so he mobilized his troops in grand style. On New Year's Day, 1845, he mounted a silver palomino and rode out through the gates of the fort at the head of a column of about 200 men. Behind him marched three drummers and a fife player, followed by 85 riflemen of various nationalities, followed by 100 Indians in Russian uniforms, then a dozen artillerymen attending a shiny brass cannon, along with a number of officers, including Field Secretary John Bidwell, Sutter's aide since 1841.

Three months later, after a disastrous campaign, Sutter returned with the remnants of his troops. The trail had led to Los Angeles, where he was captured and held prisoner for a week. Governor Micheltorena had surrendered to the Californian insurgents, whose leader, Pio Pico, had then become the new governor, and moved the capital to Los Angeles.

Although the campaign had fallen far short of his ideal of military glory, Sutter returned with a consolation prize. Before the coup, Governor Micheltorena had given him a second land grant—the Sobrante grant—consisting of 22 leagues (about 150 square miles), as payment for his services. Governor Pico let Sutter go free on the grounds that he had simply followed orders in aiding the former governor and, henceforth, would show the same commendable loyalty to the new regime. He allowed Sutter to keep all of his properties, along with his offices and titles.

As immigration continued, more women and children arrived, bringing a decided flavor of domesticity to the fort. The first white woman known to enter the Sacramento Valley was Mary Sinclair, who in 1843 arrived at the fort en route to join her husband, John, at his farm a few miles up the American River. By November 1846 there were some 60 houses in the Sacramento Valley, with 160 white men and 47 white women living in the area. In his position as *alcalde* (justice of the peace), Sutter presided at several marriages that summer. One of the women started a school, and another organized a quilting bee.

The domestic tranquility of the fort was interrupted briefly in 1846 when Lt. John Fremont and Kit Carson arrived with a group of armed men. Several weeks later Fremont returned with a group of independent settlers, also armed. Known as the Bear Flag Party, they had captured Gen. Mariano Vallejo and three high-ranking aides, whom they turned over to Sutter as prisoners. Sutter treated his prisoners with the same hospitality he showed to any gentlemen of rank, giving them his best room and inviting them to dine.

In July news arrived at Monterey that U.S. President James K. Polk had declared war against Mexico as of May 30. By this time the Bear Flag Revolt was over and California, though not yet a state, had allied itself with the United States. On the morning of July 11, the bell and drums of the fort summoned the residents to the courtyard, where the United States flag was raised with a cannon salute and appropriate military ceremony. The stars and stripes had been raised at Monterey, the traditional capital, four days earlier and at Yerba Buena and Sonoma two days earlier. For the fort's residents, this marked the end of the Mexican War, although the official conclusion, marked by the signing of the Treaty of Guadalupe Hidalgo, did not occur until a year and a half later, on February 2, 1848.

Now that California belonged to the United States, Sutter anticipated

From the early 1840s, through the first years of the Gold Rush, little permanent housing was available to immigrants to Sacramento. Building materials were scarce and expensive. The moderate climate allowed the creation of tent cities. By 1850, 125,000 people lived in California, including 100,000 settlers who had arrived during the Gold Rush. Courtesy, Norman L. Wilson

greater numbers of immigrants from the Eastern seaboard. Parties from the states were already en route by sea and land when the U.S. flag was raised in California in 1846. One such party was led by a man who would play a key role in the next few years, Mormon Elder Samuel Brannan. Five months out of New York, the ship *Brooklyn*, which had been chartered by the Mormon group, arrived at Yerba Buena shortly after the flag was raised. About half of the 240 passengers were women and children. Ten passengers had died at sea, and two babies had been born along the way.

Immigration also continued by the overland route, and many of the parties stopped by the fort to buy supplies or to settle nearby. In mid-October two gaunt, ragged men stumbled up to the gates of the fort and told of a band of immigrants trapped in the Sierras by early winter snows. Several had died and the others were starving in makeshift cabins near the lake soon to become known as Donner Lake. Sutter outfitted seven mules with flour and beef, and sent two of his Indian vaqueros with one of the men. Others in Northern California also organized rescue parties. Because of the heavy snow, the steep terrain, and the limitations of transportation on foot and by mule, it took until April to bring the last remaining survivor down from the mountains. The Donner Party had left Missouri with 87 men, women, and children. Of that number, 39 had died on the way and 48 were rescued.

On July 4, 1847, the settlers of New Helvetia celebrated their first Independence Day under the United States flag. As U.S. Indian Agent for the area, Sutter gave the following census report for his district, which included the region east of the San Joaquin and Sacramento Rivers:

Whites, Male	218	Female	71	Total	289
Indians, Tame, Male	306	Female	173	Total	479
Indians, Wild	11,224	Female	10,649	Total	21,873
Half-breed Indian Children	3	Female	7	Total	10
Sandwich Islanders, Male	4	Female	1	Total	5
Negroes, Male	1	Female	0	Total	1
Total Males:	11,756				
Total Females:	10,901		Total Population:		22,657

Sutter continued to develop the agricultural resources of the valley. After the fall's harvest, he started to build a flour mill. In preparation for next year's immigration, he laid out a plot about three miles south of the fort for what would become the city of Sutterville. To provide lumber for its houses and stores, he sent millwright James Marshall into the mountains to build a sawmill.

While Sutter developed the agricultural wealth of the area, Mormon Elder Brannan stimulated commerce. He bought property and started businesses in Yerba Buena. He started a newspaper, with Edward Kemble as reporter and editor, which not only chronicled the events of the times but provided a vehicle for advertising. He also established business relations at New Helvetia. In partnership with C.C. Smith, he opened a store just outside the walls of the fort, selling liquor, dry goods, hardware, and general merchandise.

Trade between San Francisco and New Helvetia increased with the population growth in both areas. Sutter's launch, the *Sacramento*, was manned by Indians and took about two weeks to make the 200-mile round trip. Kemble described the discomforts of river travel as he experienced them aboard the *Sacramento*.

The journey up the river was a matter of 6 or 8 days' perilous voyaging by sea and land, the perils by water arising mainly from frequently having nothing to eat and no place in which to cook it, and those by land from facing legions of mosquitoes in a similar starving condition, who greeted you with bloody bills to hospitable beds when you tied up along shore at night and lay down to sleep.

With both agricultural and commercial activity thriving and new immigration coming steadily, the future of the little settlement looked bright. In less than a decade, one man had created his own personal empire in an isolated, uncivilized, mosquito-infested wilderness. He had created a commercial and trading center, the nucleus which attracted merchants and adventurers, soldiers and missionaries, statesmen and scoundrels, men and women of all nations. He envisioned its agricultural potential. And, although he delighted in military pomp and ceremony, he maintained peaceful relations with his neighbors.

Of his own role in the establishment, Sutter wrote in his recollections, "I was everything—patriarch, priest, father, and judge."

By 1880 only the central building of Sutter's Fort remained. The rapid growth precipitated by the Gold Rush dwarfed Sutter's empire. The land occupied by the fort was sold for farming. Courtesy, California State Library Collection, Sacramento Museum and History Division (SMHD)

Chapter 2
GATEWAY TO GOLD
1849-1855

The discovery of gold in the Sierra foothills brought tens of thousands of men to California in the summer of 1849. Earlier in the year, a portion of New Helvetia had been subdivided to make a new town, Sacramento. Because of its river location, it was Sacramento, not New Helvetia, that became the center of trade and commerce.

I t was Mormon Elder Sam Brannan who sparked the Gold Rush. On May 12, 1848 he ran up and down the streets of the little seaport town of San Francisco waving his black hat in one hand and a bottle of gold dust in the other.

"Gold!" he shouted. "Gold! Gold in the American River!"

The first few flakes of the precious metal had been discovered by one of Sutter's employees, millwright James Marshall, in the foothills of the Sierras more than three months previously. Sutter had wanted lumber for the community he had laid out at Sutterville, three miles south of the fort, in anticipation of a large number of settlers immigrating to California. He sent Marshall to build a sawmill at Coloma, in the midst of the evergreen forests some 45 miles northeast of the fort. While inspecting the tail race of the nearly-completed sawmill on January 24, Marshall noticed a small, glittering object. He showed it to the cook, Jennie Wimmer, who tested it in a kettle of lye soap. After boiling all night in the lye solution, the nugget came out looking brighter than before.

Marshall then mounted a horse and rode back to the fort in pouring rain, where Sutter tested the nugget with improvised scales and assaying techniques. Later, Sutter rode back to Coloma with Marshall. Members of the work crew had found more nuggets. Fearful his workers would desert him—and his unfinished mill—to search for gold, Sutter did his best to keep the discoveries quiet.

Two weeks later, when teamster Jacob Wittmer went up to Coloma with supplies, one of Jennie's young sons told him about the find. The teamster took a nugget back to Brannan's store at Sutter's Fort and tried to purchase a bottle of brandy with it. The storekeeper, C.C. Smith, took the nugget to Sutter, who said it was genuine. Oddly, the nugget stirred little interest, until after Smith told Brannan about it—and Brannan secretly devised a plan to increase his business.

Sutter himself sent a packet of gold to the military governor at Monterey, Col. Richard B. Mason, who acknowledged its authenticity but made no move to spread the word. Brief mentions of the discovery in the San Francisco newspapers also created very little reaction.

Finally, Edward Kemble, editor of Brannan's San Francisco paper, the *California Star*, decided to take a first-hand look. He and a small party of skeptical but curious men (Sutter's embarcadero was a most unlikely place to expect a rush of commercial activity) took a boat up the Sacramento River early in May. Kemble described its primeval appearance:

> . . . *A forest of noble sycamores, dense and deep, guarding a mighty solitude like a vast army of giants in array, their bright green banners mirrored in the clear stream. Not a human habitation in sight save the Indian ferryman's hut, about the foot of J Street, and an Indian sweathouse a hundred yards, perhaps, distant above.*
>
> *Moored to the bank was an Indian canoe. A broad, well-beaten road, laid by the wheels of the "adobe cart," led back from the river's bank, the only clearing visible in all this waste and solitary place.*

From the embarcadero the road led some two miles inland to Sutter's Fort, and then it was a trek of 45 miles or so to the vicinity of the gold discovery. After inspecting the site at Coloma and finding nothing, Kemble returned to San Francisco and wrote that the rumors of gold were groundless. Then Sam Brannan, having carefully stocked his store at the fort with everything a

The discovery of gold at Sutter's sawmill on the American River on January 24, 1848, changed the history of California. James Marshall, the man who found the first nugget, posed for this photo by the abandoned mill in about 1852. Courtesy, California State University, Sacramento Collection, SMHD

Prospectors used sluices filled with flowing water to separate the heavy gold from the lighter surrounding dirt. Earth was shovelled into water passing through the sluice, and the gold, due to its weight, accumulated behind the riffles on the sluice's bottom. These men were photographed at Spanish Flat in 1852. (Windsor)

man might need for a few weeks in the mountains, arrived in San Francisco on a balmy spring day and aroused the 800 or so residents into a state of delirium.

"Gold!" he shouted again and again, waving his bottle of glittering dust. "Gold in the American River!"

People came out of their shops, houses, and tents. Skeptics turned into believers. A few men put down their tools and dashed for the boats in the harbor. More followed. The fever was contagious, and it soon became a mad scramble for the gold fields.

Within a few weeks, Sutter's embarcadero was jammed with schooners, sloops, dinghies, rowboats, and anything else with oars or sails. Brannan's store did a booming business. In the summer and fall of 1848, about 6,000 gold seekers headed for the hills, most stopping in Sacramento on the way.

After the San Franciscans and other Northern Californians, the summer's arrivals generally came from Hawaii, Oregon, and Utah. By fall, ships were bringing gold seekers from Mexico, Peru, and Chile. These adventurers were hardy young men—and a few women—who were used to a frontier existence. They were trappers, traders, soldiers, sailors, farmers, and laborers.

Along with the seekers of gold came men and women who, like Sam Brannan, seized the business opportunities that accompanied a large influx of people. They were merchants, promoters, gamblers, entertainers, and entrepreneurs. Suddenly the little settlement at the gateway to the gold fields became a lively commercial and trading center.

Because of all the activity on the banks of the Sacramento, Sutter's many creditors assumed that he had gold or goods to pay his debts. Sutter, however, had little talent for either business or prospecting. Fortuitously, Sutter's oldest son, John Augustus, Jr., arrived at the fort in the fall of 1848. The young man, a bookkeeper, spent several days looking over the fort's business records. The accounts were in disarray, but one thing was clear: Sutter owed money to almost everyone in the valley. The largest outstanding debt was that owed to the Russians for the purchase of Fort Ross in 1841.

Since Sutter owned much property but had little cash, he needed time to come up with money to repay his creditors. To buy time he granted his son power of attorney and turned over all of his property to him.

While Sutter went up to Coloma to prospect for gold, two of his associates, Sam Brannan and attorney Peter Burnett, stayed with Sutter Jr. to devise a strategy to raise money. They took four square miles of the captain's New Helvetia land grant to make a new town directly west of the fort, fronting at the embarcadero on the Sacramento River. The new town was called Sacramento, after the river that ran beside it, and it was soon to become a supply center for the influx of miners headed for the gold fields.

In December 1848, Sutter Jr. commissioned Captain William H. Warner, an Army engineer, to survey and subdivide the new city of Sacramento into lots. Together with Brannan and Burnett, the younger Sutter contracted to sell the lots to pay off his father's debts.

The sale of lots began in January 1849. Merchants Hensley and Reading, who had been doing business at Sutter's Fort for some time, built the first frame building in the new city at the corner of Front and I streets. Sam Brannan put up a frame storehouse on the corner of Front and J in February. Others also put up structures, some frame, some canvas, and some half-and-half. By April 1, 1849, about 12 buildings had been put up in the vicinity of the embarcadero, and the population of Sacramento and Sutter's Fort had reached about 150.

Sutter developed his community of Sutterville south of the present site of Sacramento. Sutter established Sutterville in 1846, hoping for an influx of American immigration after the Mexican War. Sutter's son created Sacramento and sold lots to get his father out of debt. Sacramento's proximity to the embarcadero made it more attractive to business and commercial interests. Courtesy, Sacramento City Library Collection, SMHD

In April the first of the '49ers arrived by sea. These were gold seekers from the Eastern seaboard—"back in the states." Although newspapers had carried accounts of California gold in the summer of 1848, Easterners paid little attention until President Polk, in his annual message to Congress on December 5, asserted that there was enough gold in California to pay the cost of the Mexican War "a hundred times over." Inspired by this official assurance, Easterners started packing—to the tune of "Oh, Susanna!"

But it was the middle of winter. And, two mountain ranges, a desert, and a vast expanse of prairie stood between Sacramento and the Eastern states. Wagon trains had to wait until the snow melted.

Impatient gold seekers flocked to the docks to board sailing ships. The trip around Cape Horn at the tip of the South American continent—a distance of 18,000 nautical miles—took 5 to 8 months. The alternative was to take a ship to the Isthmus of Panama, cross the isthmus by mule, and take another

Sacramento grew faster than permanent buildings could be constructed. In 1849 frame structures covered with canvas nestled under lofty cottonwoods and oaks. This style of construction grew from the scarcity of building materials. Courtesy, Norman L. Wilson

ship up the coast to San Francisco—a trip of 3 to 5 months. Lucky passengers boarded the first ocean-going steamships—introduced in 1849—which cut travel time by several weeks.

Sutter's embarcadero was the scene of hectic activity during the Gold Rush years, as it represented the head of navigation for ocean-going ships. Since captains sought to take their ships as close to the mining region as possible, most of them tied up along what is now Front Street and unloaded their cargoes on the natural levee there. Thus the community of Sacramento began with piles of merchandise left on the levee and abandoned ships tied up to the river bank. The blocks between Front and Second and I to M streets were the first to develop. The city expanded eastward, primarily along J Street.

Most of the ocean-going ships discharged their passengers at the seaport town of San Francisco, where they transferred to sloops or schooners sailing up the Sacramento River. Seizing yet another opportunity, Sam Brannan bought a Peruvian bark, the *Joven Guipuscoana*, a seagoing vessel of more than 250 tons, to carry goods and passengers between San Francisco and Sacramento. At the same time, merchants Hensley and Reading bought a Chilean brig, the *Eliodora*. Both vessels arrived in Sacramento in April, in the vanguard of the '49ers. Steamboats became a familiar sight at the embarcadero in the late fall of 1849.

The long ocean journey was debilitating, and many arrived exhausted and ill. Bayard Taylor, a *New York Tribune* reporter assigned to cover the Gold Rush, observed,

> *Three fourths of the people who settle in Sacramento City are visited by agues, diarrheas, and other reducing complaints. In summer the place is a furnace, in winter little better than a swamp; and the influx of emigrants and discouraged miners generally exceeds the demand for labor.*

In late summer the wagon trains began arriving. Taylor was struck by the travel-worn appearance of the people and animals who had journeyed overland:

> *The road to Sutter's Fort, the main streets, and the levee fronting on the embarcadero were constantly thronged with the teams of emigrants, coming in from the mountains. Such worn, weather-beaten individuals I had never before imagined. Their tents were pitched by hundreds in the thickets around the town, where they rested a few days before starting to winter in the mines and elsewhere.*
>
> *At times the levee was filled throughout its whole length by their*

teams, three or four yoke of oxen to every wagon. The beasts had an expression of patient experience which plainly showed that no roads yet to be traveled would astonish them in the least. After tugging the wagons for six months over the salt deserts of the Great Basin, climbing passes and canyons of terrible asperity in the Sierra Nevada, and learning to digest oak bark on the arid plains around the sink of Humboldt's River, it seemed as if no extremity could henceforth intimidate them.

The women who had come by the overland route appeared to have stood the hardships of the journey remarkably well, and were not half so loud as the men in their complaints.

There were major differences between the population that arrived in 1848 and that which arrived in 1849, and the social climate was quite different as a result. The gold seekers of 1848 were primarily frontiersmen. Panning for gold offered a welcome change from their usual pursuits of trapping, sailing, or ranching. Accustomed to wilderness living, they stayed healthy and enjoyed a relative freedom from crime.

Most of the '49ers came from the cities, towns, and farms of Eastern states. Unprepared for the hardships of months at sea or on the wagon trail, or for survival in primitive conditions, many fell ill and many died. A good many unscrupulous individuals were lured by the spectre of instant wealth, resulting in a high crime rate.

Since Sacramento was the common starting point for the northern mining areas, it became the outfitting place for all prospectors planning to head up any of the branches of the American, Bear, Yuba, and Feather rivers. Business activity was frenetic. On the levee bordering the embarcadero shiploads of merchandise were auctioned off, as well as used goods and anything else anyone wanted to sell. Drawing crowds by ringing bells and beating drums, auctioneers mounted their boxes and shouted out the virtues of their wares.

The horse market at 6th and K was another center of activity. Reporter Taylor described it as "one of the principal sights in the place." The oaks and

The horse market at Sixth and K streets thrived during the Gold Rush. Horses and cattle were in great demand by miners and freighters headed for the gold fields. Courtesy, Wells Fargo History Room Collection, SMHD

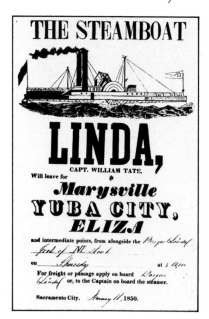

During the Gold Rush, freight and passengers from San Francisco transferred to shallow draft boats at Sacramento for the run upriver to Marysville and Red Bluff. Only the steamer *Linda* could navigate above Marysville on the Yuba River. Courtesy, Sacramento Museum and History Division Collection, SMHD

sycamores were larger and thicker than in other parts of the city. An immense oak tree in the middle of the street shaded the market ground, around which were tents of blue and white canvas. On one side was a livery stable, with stacks of hay and wheat straw nearby.

"When the market was in full blast," Taylor said, "the scene it presented was grotesque enough. There were no regulations other than the fancy of those who had animals to sell; every man was his own auctioneer."

Just as the Sacramento River was the main artery connecting Sacramento to San Francisco and the rest of the world by sea, J Street became the artery connecting the city to the interior and points east. Ox teams, mule teams, horses and foot traffic headed out J Street, which was perpendicular to Front Street and the levee and ran due east from the river. Upon reaching 12th, traffic destined for the northern mines in the vicinity of Auburn, Grass Valley, and Nevada City turned left and headed north, taking Lisle's ferry or, later, Lisle's Bridge (site of the present 12th Street Bridge) across the American River.

Until the coming of the railroad, nearly all of the gold that was brought out of the northern mines came into Sacramento over J Street. Thousands and thousands of dollars' worth of gold dust and nuggets were brought into town by miners on foot, by mule and horseback, by wagons, and by teams.

The residents of the new city of Sacramento celebrated the Fourth of July in 1849 by hosting a grand ball in the newly built, three-story City Hotel on Front Street, sparing no expense to provide a lavish entertainment befitting their new and lively prosperity. The organizers scoured the countryside to find ladies to grace the ballroom floor. About 200 men paid to attend, and 18 women honored them with their presence. One of the men, Dr. John Morse, a physician and journalist, described the women as "not all amazons, but replete with all the adornments and graces that belong to bold and enterprising pioneers of a new country."

The universal entertainment was gambling. One of the early '49ers, James Lee, put a few poles on the ground on J Street and covered them with a canvas sail from an abandoned schooner. With a few planks of wood for a table, some boxes to sit on, and a deck of cards, he improvised the first gaming rendezvous. Because of the smell of the canvas, the establishment soon

Lisle's Bridge, one of the first in Sacramento, was located over the American River at the present 12th Street. The bridge linked Sacramento to the northern mines. This bridge replaced an earlier ferry at the same site. Courtesy, California State Library Collection, SMHD

acquired the nickname, "The Stinking Tent." Others soon followed suit, and gambling halls proliferated. Zadock Hubbard, a '49er, erected a round tent, 50 feet in diameter, also on J. Inside it boasted an elaborately decorated bar, paintings of women in a variety of poses and states of dress (or undress), live music, and every kind of gambling.

Games of monte, faro, and poker drew huge crowds of players and onlookers. Dr. Morse lamented the irresistible lure of Lady Luck:

> *The toilers of the country, including traders, mechanics, and speculators, lawyers, doctors, and some apostate ministers, concentrated at this gambling focus, like insects around a lighted candle at night; and like insects, seldom left the delusive glare until scorched and consumed by the fires of destruction.*

Throughout the summer the activity on the embarcadero and in the city increased. Newly-built steamships joined schooners, sloops, and sailing vessels on the water. Ships continued to arrive daily, and many were abandoned or sold as all hands headed for the mines.

Trading and commercial activity dominated the day, while music and gambling continued far into the night. Outside of the gambling halls the city was dark, for candles were scarce and most residents went to bed when the sun went down. But the bright lights and live music of the halls on the levee attracted crowds. Musicians of all sorts added their sounds to the bustle. Reporter Bayard Taylor described the cacophony of sound that resulted:

> *The door of many a gambling-hell on the levee, and in J and K Streets, stands invitingly open; the wail of torture from innumerable musical instruments peals from all quarters through the fog and darkness. Full bands, each playing different tunes discordantly, are stationed in front of the principal establishments, and as these happen to be near together, the mingling of the sounds in one horrid, ear-splitting, brazen chaos would drive frantic a man of delicate nerve.*

George Cooper sketched this view of Sacramento City in the fall of 1849. The city grew along the banks of the Sacramento River and out along J Street in a "T" configuration. Sacramento commanded such attention during the Gold Rush that Cooper's view was copied by artists all over the world. Over 50 different versions of this sketch have been found. Courtesy, Lucinda M. Woodward

Black singers were especially popular. "Some of the establishments have small companies of Ethiopian melodists, who nightly call upon 'Susanna!' and entreat to be carried back to Old Virginny," Taylor reported. "The crowd of listeners is often so great as to injure the business of the gamblers."

The exuberance of the Gold Rush period lasted just a few years. By the middle of the 1850s most of the loose gold had been picked up from the streams and mountainsides, and pick-and-shovel prospecting no longer provided easy rewards. Panning lost its luster. Men formed into companies to invest in more sophisticated equipment such as hydraulic hoses and hardware. Effective mining operations required capital.

For every miner who struck it rich, dozens returned from the hills disillusioned. Yet in the aggregate, the amount of gold retrieved by the pick-and-shovel miners was fantastic—over $10 million worth in 1849; over $81 million in the peak year of 1852. (And that was in 1850-era dollars!)

California's mineral wealth made Easterners sit up and take notice. Politically, the golden harvest was a powerful argument for California's claim to

By the mid 1850s most of the surface gold had been picked up, and placer mining was no longer profitable. Big business entered gold mining to provide the heavy equipment necessary for hydraulic and hard rock mining. The days of the mining camp made up of tents gave way to more substantial housing. Courtesy, Norman L. Wilson

statehood. Even more important than the immediate economic or political effect, the lure of gold brought immigrants—people to settle and build farms, businesses, and homes in the new land.

Even before the onslaught of 1849, businessmen in the vicinity of New Helvetia had begun laying the groundwork for a permanent community. Orderly growth would require a system of government. In the early spring of 1849, in preparation for the expected influx of gold-seekers from the Eastern states, Sam Brannan and a dozen merchants met under an oak tree at the foot of I Street to draft a code of laws.

They had just vanquished a rival town's bid for the focus of commercial development. The conflict had originated because George McDougal, a merchant who had set up a store-ship on the embarcadero, got into a dispute with Sutter Jr. and moved his ship with all of its merchandise to Sutterville (Captain Sutter's first choice for a town site). McDougal persuaded the elder Sutter and several other Sutterville proprietors to lure the Sacramento merchants to Sutterville by offering them 80 lots free of charge. Brannan and his associates craftily reported this offer to Sutter Jr., who then retaliated by offering the merchants 500 lots to stay in the location fronting on the embarcadero. Having secured this generous endowment, the merchants got together to create an orderly system for the conduct of business and the development of the community.

For most of the previous decade California had been governed under the autocratic Spanish system, with total power in each district vested in one man, the alcalde. Captain Sutter of New Helvetia had been the alcalde for the entire north central district of California, but when the United States flag was raised at Sutter's fort in the summer of 1846, the democratic system was superimposed on the Spanish system, and the resulting compromise worked very well as long as Sutter commanded a loyal following in his district.

Just two years later, inundated with newcomers and overwhelmed by the pressures of creditors, Sutter abdicated, leaving his affairs in the hands of his son and two advisors, Sam Brannan and Peter Burnett. As an attorney, Burnett had a thorough grounding in the theory and application of democratic law. As a practical businessman, Brannan appreciated the need for a stable system of government.

The '49ers, familiar with the conduct of self-government in the East, readily agreed to the plans set forth by the group that had met under the oak tree. In July of 1849 nine men were elected to the newly-formed city council. The council members elected William Stout president, but Stout left town

Facing page, top and above: Ships converted into storehouses lined the steamboat landing in the early 1850s. The steamers that made daily runs between Sacramento and San Francisco landed here beginning in late 1849. The embarcadero extended from I Street south to about M Street. These two views decorated a folding lettersheet that a lonely miner used to send a message home. Courtesy, Norman L. Wilson

John A. Sutter, Jr., arrived at New Helvetia in August 1848. That year he received his father's power of attorney and laid out and sold lots in the new city of Sacramento in order to pay his father's debts. He is considered the founder of Sacramento, and his grave is in the Sacramento City Cemetery. Courtesy, California State Library

three weeks later, and the council elected General A.M. Winn, land agent and civic activist, to replace him. The council's first task was to draft a city charter to submit to the voters.

The councilmen presented the newly-drafted charter to the voters on September 20. It was soundly defeated—only 381 voting for it; 527 voted against it. Gambling was probably a factor in the charter's defeat. Gambling was the most popular occupation in the city, and the gambling interests did not want regulation. The councilmen rallied their friends, formed a "Law and Order" party, and amended their proposed charter. Campaigning for its passage, they circulated a handbill promoting the concept of self-government:

> *Being republicans in principle, and having every confidence in the ability of the people to govern themselves, we again request the residents of Sacramento City to meet and to declare what they wish the City Council to do. The Health and Safety of our City demand immediate action on your part, for in our primitive condition and in the absence of Legislative authority we can, in fact, be of no service to you without your confidence and consent.*

The second charter election, held October 13, succeeded. Although almost as many as before voted against it, over twice as many turned out in its favor. The amended charter carried by a majority of 808 to 513.

Thus, 1849 was an eventful year. The city had established its location, elected a governing body and passed a code of laws. Early the next year the newly-constituted state government ratified the city's efforts. Following the legislature's acceptance of the Sacramento City Charter in February, the city was officially incorporated on March 18, 1850. Voters in April elected their first mayor, Hardin Bigelow, under the new charter.

While the city was getting organized, a struggle ensued over property rights. Many of the '49ers put up tents or shanties wherever they found a clearing. After one of the newcomers, Dr. Charles Robinson, built a shanty on the levee without paying for the land, the city council had it torn down. In protest Robinson organized a squatters' association and, with reporter James McClatchy, started a newspaper, the *Settlers and Miners Tribune.*

The squatters argued that the land did not belong to Sutter, but to the United States government, and therefore could be claimed by anyone who occupied and improved it.

But Sutter Jr. and the citizens who had bought lots from him based their claim to ownership on the validity of Sutter's Spanish land grant. As part of the Mexican Treaty of 1848, the United States had guaranteed that Californians holding land under the Spanish-Mexican system would continue to be protected in their titles.

The land dispute was interrupted briefly by the flood of January 1850. As the waters rose in the city, many squatters put up tents and shanties on the high ground near the fort and on the levee. They stayed on the levee after the water subsided, obstructing the landing of merchandise and exasperating the merchants and bankers, who then took matters into their own hands. Led by Sam Brannan, they marched en masse to the foot of I Street where Dr. Robinson had started another house. They ripped up the floor and foundation, then moved on to tear down other squatters' buildings. While the squatters threatened and cursed, a gathering crowd of onlookers cheered and laughed wildly as each shanty tumbled to the ground.

In May two early Sacramentans filed suit against one of the squatters,

John T. Madden, in the newly-organized recorder's court, which had jurisdiction over matters pertaining to city ordinances. When Judge B.F. Washington ruled against Madden, he appealed to the county court.

Three months later the case went before a county court judge, E.J. Willis, who sustained the lower court's verdict and denied Madden's request to appeal to the state supreme court. The squatters then circulated a large handbill listing their grievances and threatening armed resistance: "If there is no other appeal from Judge Willis, the settlers and others have deliberately resolved to appeal to arms, and protect their sacred rights, if needs be, with their lives."

On August 14, an armed band of 40 to 50 squatters led by Dr. Robinson and another '49er, James Maloney, marched on foot and on horseback to the levee, and then to the corner of 4th and J, where they were met by Mayor Hardin Bigelow, Sheriff Joseph McKinney, and a crowd of citizens. When the mayor ordered the squatters to drop their arms and disperse, several shots rang out. Bigelow fell from his horse, wounded by four shots. The city assessor, J.W. Woodland, who had been standing near Bigelow, was killed instantly. One of the squatters was killed, one citizen was severely wounded, and a little boy was also injured. Maloney's horse was shot out from under him, and when he attempted to escape through an alley, he was shot in the head and died instantly. Robinson, wounded in the leg, was arrested and taken to the prison ship moored at the embarcadero.

With one of their leaders dead and the other one under arrest, the squatters quickly scattered. General A.M. Winn, president of the city council, put

Many versions of the 1849 Cooper lithograph, such as this one, appeared during the second half of the 19th century. Most of these received embellishments that bore little resemblance to the city's actual appearance. The fanciful French lithograph on the back of the dust jacket was also based on Cooper's view. Courtesy, National Archives

the city under martial law and recruited 500 volunteers to keep order. The night passed without incident.

The following day Sheriff McKinney and a small posse confronted a group of about a dozen squatters at the Five-Mile House in Brighton. In the gunfight that followed, the sheriff and three of the squatters were killed.

With a semblance of calm restored, Sacramento citizens counted the casualties: five squatters and two citizens dead, three squatters and five citizens wounded. Two widows were left mourning. Mayor Bigelow never quite recovered from his wounds and died of cholera in San Francisco a few months later.

Following the Squatters' Riot the courts continued to wrestle with land title problems, although, as a practical matter, the issue had been settled. Ownership derived from Spanish land grants would be respected, while those wishing to build in the city of Sacramento would be required to buy or lease the land from its title holder.

In criminal matters as well as civil disputes citizens quickly set up judicial procedures to meet the rapidly changing times. Practical considerations often ranked foremost, for the great influxes of population of 1848 and 1849 occurred just as California was changing over from the Spanish alcalde system to the Anglo-Saxon court system.

During the Gold Rush of 1848, the legal system operated informally for the most part, for the immigrants of that year were primarily frontiersmen. Physician Morse spoke highly of the law-abiding spirit which prevailed:

> *Such was the marvelous spirit of honesty which prevailed that neither goods nor gold dust were watched with the least care or consideration. Miners coming to town, freighted with bags of the valuable ore, stowed away their treasure as indifferently as they did their hats and boots.*
>
> *There was really no government, no acknowledged standard to regulate the concessions and mutual forbearances of a common intercourse and neighborhood relations, and yet no person was ungoverned, and the spirit of accommodation sat in radiance upon all of the transactions of a mass thus singularly blended.*

One murder trial did take place at Sutter's Fort in 1848. That winter two merchants got into an argument and one of them attacked the other with an axe. Backed up against a wall, merchant Charles Pickett drew his gun and fired, killing his attacker instantly. Although it was clearly self-defense, merchant Sam Brannan insisted on pressing charges against Pickett. None of the fort residents wanted to bring Pickett to trial, but they allowed Brannan to set up a court hearing whereby Brannan served as both judge and prosecuting attorney.

On the appointed day Pickett appeared in court—a room at the fort—with his counsel. Captain Sutter and 11 other fort residents made up the jury. When everyone had assembled, the sheriff came in with drinks and cigars for all. By the time Brannan wound up the case for the prosecution, it was after midnight and two jurors were asleep. Pickett had to sum up the defense for himself, because, it was reported, the counsel for the defense was "too far gone to take any further part in the proceedings."

Although the jury deliberated into the wee hours of the morning, it could not agree on a verdict. A little later, Pickett was given a new trial, conducted with a little more sobriety, and was acquitted.

The city government building was located at the corner of Front and I streets from 1854-1894. The city water reservoir on top of the building delivered a gravity flow of water that was a significant factor in controlling fires. Pressurized water mains made this system obsolete by the 1870s. Courtesy, Sacramento Museum and History Division Collection, SMHD

Although the conduct of justice was somewhat haphazard, it proved fairly effective because old timers and newcomers alike generally respected each other's rights to personal property and safety. But with the new wave of immigrants from the Atlantic seaboard in 1849, thefts and petty crimes increased. Problems of law and order multiplied while the city, county, and state struggled simultaneously to get their legal systems organized.

The Sacramento court handed down its first criminal conviction on November 8, 1849. The defendant was fined $515 for stealing a $20 heifer. Throughout that exceptionally wet and rainy winter, the newspapers reported robberies, burglaries, thefts, arson, assaults, and street shootings. On February 24, 1850, a 20-year-old Englishman, Frederick J. Roe, and a stranger from the mines quarreled at a monte table. When a local citizen tried to stop the fight, Roe pulled a gun and killed him.

An officer arrested Roe immediately and took him to the station house at 2nd and J. An angry crowd gathered. Fed up with the recent spate of lawlessness, the crowd appointed a 12-man jury and conducted a hearing on the spot. When they returned a verdict of guilty, the crowd cheered and stampeded for the station house. With battering rams improvised from awning posts, the crowd bashed in the door, rushed past the deputy sheriff, and unshackled Roe. With his hands and feet tied, the prisoner was marched to the large oak tree at the horse market at 6th and K, where a scaffold had already been erected. A minister said a few last words to the prisoner and to the crowd, which had swelled to about 5,000 (practically everyone in town). A slip-noose was placed around the prisoner's neck while the other end of the rope was thrown over a sturdy branch and pulled taut. The lynching served as a warning that citizens would not tolerate crime.

The next hanging did not occur until a year and a half later. When three men were sentenced to be hanged on August 22, 1851, a scaffold was erected at 4th and O. Two of the men were hanged legally, but the governor had granted a reprieve to the third. The crowd, believing this man to be even more guilty than his two companions, seized him from the jail and hanged him as well. Immediately afterwards, a committee met to draw up a statement ex-

The Sacramento City Hall and Water Works building, built in 1854 at the corner of Front and I streets, housed the Sacramento Police Department. In 1909 the building was replaced by the present City Hall on I Street between 9th and 10th streets. Courtesy, California State Library Collection, SMHD

plaining their actions. Lynchings, it said, were a warning to wrongdoers that justice would prevail.

In 1853 a scaffold was erected near Sutter's Fort for the hanging of three members of a gang who had murdered a fourth gang member. It was used on two more occasions in 1856: once, in February, when a Chinese man, Ah Chung, was hanged for stabbing and killing a Chinese woman, Ah Lee; and again in June, when a groom, Samuel Garrett, was hanged for shooting his father-in-law in a dispute over the couple's elopement. By 1858, public hanging was banned by the state legislature.

While dealing severely with crimes of violence, the frontier society was quite tolerant of matters which, although legally coming under the criminal code, resulted in neither personal harm nor property damage. Prostitution, for example, was not treated as a criminal matter during the city's first few decades. Many prostitutes were quite open about their profession. They were seldom arrested, but enjoyed the same police protection as other citizens. Some of the proprietors of the houses were talented businesswomen like Johanna Hiegel, who bought and managed property. She ran a cigar business and a house of ill repute on 2nd Street between I and J for nearly 30 years, beginning in 1854.

For the women, a house often offered security, protection, and the companionship of women in the same profession. For the men, a house served as a social center. The parlor was a central gathering place where men could enjoy drinks, music, and female companionship. In 1855 the state legislature made it a misdemeanor to keep or reside in a "house of ill-fame," but there were no attempts to enforce the law. In 1872 a Sacramento County grand jury recommended that prohibitory laws be repealed on the grounds that "laws unenforced are of more damaging influence than any violation of law in detail."

By the 1870s, however, the trend was toward greater regulation. A city ordinance was passed to prevent women from soliciting customers in view of the public. A few days after the legislature adjourned in April of 1872, the newly-elected chief of police, Matt Karcher, sent his officers out to notify "all keepers of houses of ill-repute" that they must "keep their doors closed and refrain from standing on the sidewalks or in the doorways to induce people to enter."

Most of the arrests in the first few decades were for drunk and disorderly behavior. Women as well as men were taken to the police station for fighting and swearing. Female prisoners cooked and cleaned, while the males worked on the chain gang, maintaining the streets and levees.

An abandoned sailing ship served as one of the city's first prisons. The barque *La Grange* of Massachusetts had arrived at the embarcadero in October 1849. Upon reaching the city, a crew member recalled, the company "sold the copper off the vessel for sieves to gold rockers, the sails for roofs of houses, and the running rigging for lashings for wagons, and the galley for a lawyer's office."

The County of Sacramento bought what was left of the ship and moored it at the mouth of the American River. The hold was partitioned into cells and a superstructure was added topside, making it ready for use in the summer of 1850. Although a new courthouse and jail building was completed in 1855, the *La Grange* continued in service until it sank during a heavy rainstorm in 1859.

Within a few short years of its founding, the city had established orderly procedures for keeping the peace and dealing with offenders. The speed with which this was accomplished is all the more remarkable considering its chaotic beginning, characterized by the sudden influx of thousands of young, exuberant males attracted by the possibility of obtaining great wealth, and uninhibited by traditional constraints of family and community.

Unlike many other regions which had similar beginnings, the Sacramento region rapidly developed a cultural, religious, and educational life completely inconsistent with the rougher elements of society. It was this development which tempered the frontier society associated with the excesses of the Gold Rush.

In the 1850s Sacramento used the barque *La Grange* as a floating prison ship. The jail operated until the ship sank in 1859. The hull was washed away in the flood of 1861-1862. Courtesy, California State Library Collection, SMHD

Chapter 3
RISING ABOVE DISASTER
1849-1890

While facing a series of disasters reminiscent of Biblical scourges, first generation Sacramentans not only coped with their physical environment but also developed an educational, social, cultural, and religious life reflecting democratic values and spiritual ideals. They brought order and city services to the young community, and, by the 1890s, took great pride in their city's progress.

Duuring Sacramento's first three years, it was nearly wiped out by a succession of disasters: disease, flood, and fire.

Many of the immigrants of 1849 arrived in the city broke, hungry, and exhausted by months of travel. They fell easy prey to colds, flu, diarrhea, and sometimes fatal fevers. On August 20 General A.M. Winn, president of the city council, called together friends who were members of the Odd Fellows, an international fraternal and benevolent association.

"A dreadful calamity has overtaken us," Winn told them. "Hundreds are lying sick, rolled in their filthy blankets, without wife, children or friends to nurse them while sick, or bury them when dead."

The Odd Fellows took it upon themselves to visit the sick and raise money for rough pine coffins. As December rainstorms turned the young city into a swampy morass, hundreds of miners came down from the hills to escape the Sierra snows. The thousands already in distress for want of food, shelter, and medical care now found themselves crowded by more of the same.

The city council sent Winn to ask the U.S. military governor in Monterey for federal relief funds. It was to no avail. Bitterly, Dr. John Morse, one of the founders of the Odd Fellows in Sacramento, reported that Winn's mission was a failure: "General Bennett Riley, the Military Governor of the territory, did not consider himself in possession of the right to make such an appropriation of the national funds."

The next fall another epidemic hit the city. When the river steamer, the *New World*, arrived at the embarcadero on October 19, 1850, with the welcome news of California's admission to the union, it also brought the germination of another disaster. At dawn on the day after the ship arrived, someone found one of its passengers lying on the levee in the last convulsive stages of cholera, a highly contagious disease which caused diarrhea, vomiting, chills, and fever. Cholera struck fear into the hearts of the people because of its sudden onset and, according to Dr. Morse, "the malignant and hopeless rapidity with which it hurried its victims into eternity."

As the disease spread quickly, people left town in every direction, reducing the population to about one fifth of its former number. Dr. Morse and the other physicians in the city stayed behind to tend the sick and dying. Nearly a third of the doctors—17—lost their lives, and another third came down with the disease but recovered. The death toll numbered in the hundreds, and many were buried without ceremony in a common grave in the city cemetery at Riverside and Broadway.

The cholera epidemic exposed the need for public health measures— clean water, sanitation, and sewage disposal—but it took several decades to solve these problems. For years the primary weapon, often the only weapon, in the battle against disease was the use of strong disinfectants. (Newspapers urged citizens to pour them into their privies, septic tanks, and any pools of stagnant water.) Sacramento in 1862 became one of the first municipalities to create a city board of health.

The epidemic lasted about 20 days. As soon as it subsided, many who had fled the city returned. Merchants reopened their businesses and resumed trade with the mines. Dr. Morse commented on the city's speedy recuperation, helped by a mild winter: "The broken and beautiful winter that followed imparted a vitality to the town that could not have been anticipated by one who contemplated its destiny through the gloomy scenes of the October previous."

Another kind of disaster almost destroyed the city just one year after its

Facing page: The use of wood frame buildings and the city's proximity to the rivers caused a series of disasters in Sacramento in the 1850s and 1860s. The city was flooded and burned several times until levees and brick buildings were built. This is the fire of November 1852. Courtesy, California State Library

Looking south from the Southern Pacific shops across Sutter's Slough this view shows the low terrain that made Sacramento vulnerable to floods during the 19th century. Third Street is at the right and I Street runs along the other side of the slough. Courtesy, David Joslyn Collection, SMHD

founding. The rain which had aggravated the '49ers' misery continued through January 1850. On January 8 the American River overflowed into Sutter Slough, a finger of the Sacramento River extending inland to 6th Street between I Street and the American. From the slough the floodwater poured into the city, washing away tents, wagons, livestock, and merchandise. Homes and stores were flooded and boats were used to rescue people from their homes.

Dr. Morse helped rescue a number of patients from a canvas shelter which had served as a hospital. Their condition revealed grievous neglect. They had not been bathed in weeks. One man, wrapped from head to toe in a filthy blanket, died shortly after being removed from the boat. "The blanket was with difficulty detached," Dr. Morse reported, "and when drawn off presented a shirtless body already partially devoured by an immense bed of maggots."

Those who were neither bedridden nor engaged in rescue operations defied the elements with hysterical merrymaking. "The city seemed almost mad with boisterous frolic, with the most irresistible disposition to revel in all the joking, laughing, talking, drinking, swearing, dancing, and shouting," Dr. Morse recalled. "A man who would purposely roll into the water that he might share the general laugh that was entailed upon one who had accidentally fallen in would not wet the sole of his foot or disturb a joke to save a barrel of his pork that was being carried off by the current."

As the waters receded the people began rebuilding. One of the citizens, Hardin Bigelow, urged the city council to build a levee for flood protection, but his entreaties were ignored. Like gamblers, most of the people simply refused to believe that such a disaster would ever happen again.

Blue skies and sunshine contributed to the feeling of security, but in March it started raining again. The rain hastened the melting of the Sierra snowpack and the rivers rose again. Bigelow recruited a handful of men to build up the river banks with mud and rock at every low point. The makeshift levees held, and Dr. Morse reported, "To the utter astonishment of all, he saved the town from a severe inundation."

At the city election in April, the voters elected Hardin Bigelow mayor— and his program to build permanent levees finally gained support.

The next disaster was the fire of 1852. Accidental fires were common, for people used candles and kerosene for light, and the wood and canvas buildings burned easily. Early in 1850 citizens had organized a volunteer fire department—Mutual Hook and Ladder No. 1. Soon they added three engine companies and built cisterns at street intersections along J Street to store water for the pumpers.

Shortly after 11 p.m. on November 2, 1852, someone noticed smoke from a millinery shop on the north side of town (J near 4th) and sounded the alarm. Volunteer firemen responded promptly, but by the time they arrived, the strong north wind was fanning the flames to the south, east, and west. In the next seven hours the entire business district was demolished and hundreds of residents were left homeless.

The newspaper office of the *Sacramento Union,* founded in 1851, was destroyed, but staff members managed to save a press, some type, and some paper. Missing only one edition, the *Union* reappeared a day later to tell the story.

San Francisco and other Northern California cities came to Sacramento's aid. Within a month most homes and businesses had been rebuilt. And lessons had been learned: the new commercial buildings were made of brick instead of wood. Two years later on July 13, 1854, when another major fire destroyed over 200 frame houses and badly damaged many of the brick buildings, many merchants put metal shutters on their windows for added protection.

The volunteer fire department served as a men's social club as well as a protective organization. Occasionally, however, the friendly competition

Without an effective water supply the fire of November 1852 nearly destroyed Sacramento. Local citizens responded to the crisis with spirit. Within a few days new buildings had been raised, and stores were back in business. Courtesy, California State Library Collection, SMHD

The *Sacramento Union* is the oldest surviving newspaper in the West. The paper's original office, shown here, was located at 21 J Street. This building was destroyed during the fire of November 2, 1852, but the paper only missed one edition. Courtesy, California State Library

which sprang up between companies got out of hand. In one instance, Confidence Engine Company No. 1 and Knickerbocker Company No. 5 raced each other to a fire at the new Jefferson school. En route, they had to cross a narrow bridge over a slough. They reached the bridge at the same time and collided, knocking one of the engines into the slough. While the two companies' volunteers engaged in fistfights, the school burned to the ground.

In 1872 the people of Sacramento voted to replace the volunteers with a paid fire department. And so, beginning officially on January 1, 1873, fire protection became a permanent function of city government.

Early on, citizens combined private and public resources in dealing with a major element in the prevention and control of disasters: water. Situated at the junction of two rivers, Sacramento had plenty of water, but the water was below city level and required pumps to make it available for homes, businesses, and fire fighting.

The first commercial supplier of water simply bailed it out of the river and into his water cart, then peddled it door to door. Soon a competitor rigged up a suction pump on the bank just upstream from I Street and pumped the water into an elevated tank, from which he loaded his water carts by gravity flow.

The Young America Fire House, near the corner of 10th and I streets, was staffed with volunteers at the time of this July 1857 photograph. The cupola from this engine house is now located at the fire station near H and Carlson streets across from California State University, Sacramento. Courtesy, California State Library Collection, SMHD

In 1854 the city completed a three-story water works building at the foot of I Street. The main part of the building was the city hall. On the roof were two six-foot-deep tanks, which held 240,000 gallons of water, pumped up from the river and distributed throughout the city by gravity flow.

River water in the early years was clear, but by the 1860s hydraulic mining in the mountains was washing tons of sediment down to the valley floor. The brownish-tan color of a glass of river water resembled a shot of whiskey, and Sacramentans jokingly referred to it as "Sacramento Straight." The problem was not resolved until 1923, when a new filtration plant was built to purify the water.

Waste disposal posed another problem for the young city. The traditional method was to construct a small shack, or privy, fitted with a seat inside, over a hole in the ground. When the hole was filled with waste matter, another was dug and the privy moved over it. A promising innovation made its appearance in the 1870s: the water closet. The theory was simple. Water could be used to flush human waste into a sewer system. If the water closet was installed indoors, it would eliminate the need for bedpans and chamber pots, and the walk to the cold, dark outhouse on a rainy night.

Yet physicians viewed the device with caution, largely because the early toilets were difficult to clean and when flushed allowed sewer gases to come up into the home. Dr. F.W. Hatch, city health officer, warned that many of the water closets in hotels and private homes were "badly constructed; for the most part cheap and inefficient concerns; and seldom properly ventilated."

Other kinds of waste also created noxious smells. Several dairies, a number of hog yards, a glue factory, and several slaughterhouses were located within city limits. In addition, there was the constant traffic of horses and livestock on the city streets.

Because Sacramento was built on flat land, water in the open drainage ditches often backed up, forming reeking, stagnant pools. Summer breezes wafting into the city passed over such a pool at the intersection of Broadway and 18th Street, and the area became known as "the terror of the south winds."

By the 1870s Sutter Lake, also known as China Lake, was another source of repulsive odors. The Chinese who had settled along I Street, bordering the south shore, emptied their refuse and the wastewater from their laundry houses into the lake. On the northern shore, the railroad shops also used the lake as a waste disposal area. Often the stench was so nauseous that passersby needed to hold their noses. And once the lake became so clogged with oily debris from the shops that it caught fire and burned. The lake remained a problem until 1906, when Southern Pacific filled it in.

Another flood devastated the city in 1861. Originally the American River had formed a U-shaped curve toward the town in the vicinity of 28th and B, where Sutter had first landed. About mid-morning on December 9, 1861, the levee there gave way and the river overflowed. It spilled into Smith's Pomological Gardens, flooding the orchards, and flowed on in the direction of the R Street levee. That levee—built to put the Sacramento Valley Railroad above the waterway known as Burns' Slough—prevented the floodwaters from escaping. The city sent a chain gang to blast out a section of the levee and the water rushed through the opening with such force that it took half a dozen homes with it.

The flood of 1861 revealed the inadequacy of the city's rudimentary sewer system. As a result, Dr. F.W. Hatch organized a City Board of Health in 1862, which initiated the construction of a centrally planned sewer system

Photographer Charles Weed captured this image of Sacramento's greatest flood in January 1862. Boats became a common form of transportation through Sacramento's streets during each flood. After the 1862 flood the City of Sacramento moved the river's mouth, and in 1868 the city literally straightened out the troublesome U-shaped curve of the American River. Courtesy, Ralph Shaw Collection, SMHD

modeled after the one in London.

Within a few years the city dug new channels for the American River: one to straighten out the troublesome curve; the other to relieve pressure at the mouth of the American by bringing it into the Sacramento River at a point about a quarter of a mile north of the original junction.

Perhaps the most remarkable feat in solving the problem of flooding was the raising of the streets, sidewalks, and buildings of the entire downtown area. Following months of controversy, merchants and citizens undertook to raise 12 blocks of I, J, and K streets to a height of 12 to 15 feet above their original level. Early in 1864 they started building 10-foot-high brick bulkheads along the streets. Using wheelbarrows, picks and shovels, one-horse dump carts, and small team wagons, they hauled in dirt to fill the roads; they built wooden sidewalks to match the new grade; they raised buildings, including the County Courthouse, on jackscrews and built new foundations.

During the next nine years, streets, buildings, and sections of sidewalks reached different heights at different times. Unwary pedestrians sometimes stepped off an upper level sidewalk onto a part of the sidewalk some eight or

Workers and citizens posed about 1870 for a picture of the raising of the Sacramento County Courthouse located at the northwest corner of 7th and I streets. The entire building, along with many others in the city's central business district, was raised and given a new foundation during the street raising that occurred in Sacramento in the 1860s and 1870s. This project lifted Sacramento above the level of flood waters. Courtesy, Ralph Shaw Collection, SMHD

ten feet below. In 1865 the section of 2nd Street between J and K was raised, along with the board sidewalk. The owners of the Union and Orleans hotels, however, had been unable to raise their buildings because of rain. During the legislative session, lawmakers reached the entryways to their hotels by going through a hatchway in the sidewalk and down a wooden ladder.

Despite the inconvenience, Sacramentans persevered with good spirits and tenacious optimism. By 1873, they had succeeded in raising a city.

And, even while struggling for survival, Sacramentans worked to make their city the cultural and humanitarian heart of the West.

While Sacramento started out as merely the inland transfer point for goods and supplies, it quickly became a center for the development and diffusion of cultural values as well—education, humanitarianism, fine arts, and spirituality.

Newspapers proliferated. As soon as the rush of 1848 was well under way, Sam Brannan moved the *California Star*'s handpress, type, and paper to Sutter's Fort and began publishing the *Placer Times*. A number of '49ers brought more newspaper publishing equipment and started other sheets. In

By 1857, only nine years after the discovery of gold, Sacramento was a flourishing city. Sacramento had a railroad along R Street, a city hall at Front and I streets, and levees along the rivers. George Baker created this lithograph, "The City of the Plain," in 1857. Courtesy, Lucinda M. Woodward

This collection of early Sacramento business cards expresses the humor of the day. These were stock cards on which different businesses would print their names. Courtesy, Norman L. Wilson

The first school building built and owned by the city was dedicated in January 1855 at the corner of 10th and H streets. A later school, the East Sacramento Grammar School (shown here), was located at 39th and J streets, the present site of Sacred Heart Church. Courtesy, Sacramento Museum and History Division Collection, SMHD

1851 the *Placer Times* and one of the newer papers, the *Transcript*, found themselves in a rate war. Both papers reduced advertising charges so much that they were unable to pay their expenses; they asked the printers to help out by taking a pay cut. The printers countered by striking, and then started their own paper, the *Sacramento Union*.

During the dispute between the squatters and the city, the squatters had published their own newspaper, the *Settlers and Miners Tribune*, edited by '49er James McClatchy. Following the Squatter Riots, McClatchy continued his journalistic career on various other publications. In 1857 he accepted a position as head reporter for a new daily paper, the *Sacramento Bee*. Both the *Bee* and the *Union* have been in continuous publication since their founding.

One enterprising teacher started a school in the summer of 1849, but it folded after a few weeks due to a scarcity of students. Several private schools were started in the next few years and, thanks to an increase of children in town, they met with more success.

As soon as the state provided funding for a public school system, Sacramento opened its first public school (February 20, 1854, at 5th and K). About 50 boys and 40 girls, most between seven and nine, arrived for classes. Enroll-

The Mary J. Watson school was built on one of the public squares which Sutter, Jr., donated to the city. This square was bounded by I, J, 15th, and 16th streets. In 1872 the city donated the land for the school. In the 1920s the school was replaced by the Memorial Auditorium. John Todd, a popular Sacramento photographer of the 1870s, took this picture. Courtesy, Argus Books Collection, SMHD

Perry's Seminary for Young Ladies was built in 1867 on I Street between 10th and 11th streets. In 1876, 190 young women studied in high school and college preparatory classes at the school. The building was torn down in 1931. Courtesy, California State Library Collection, SMHD

ment nearly doubled within the first week, so another room was rented. By July a school census counted 261 students in public schools and 250 in private schools.

By state policy, a separate school was provided for black students. In 1872 there were, according to the census, 89 black children of school age, two-thirds of whom were attending school. In the 1860s and 1870s the city had a large Chinese population, primarily due to railroad construction. Members of the Methodist and Congregational churches started schools to teach English and Bible studies to the Chinese, both children and adults. By the 1870s there were over 4,000 school-age children in the city, half of whom attended public schools. They were diffused among 12 school buildings, including the newly-opened high school which had four classrooms, a library, and a laboratory.

When not in school, children entertained themselves with the materials at hand. Sometimes they rolled barrel hoops along the bumpy streets, using a stick to keep them upright. They went to the levee and watched the trains, teams, and ships. They carved whistles out of wood. Using a tin can and a piece of string, they made an instrument called a "Devil's Fiddle"; it made a noise so dreadful that, according to one witness, "it caused horses to start, strong men to turn pale, and ladies to faint." Swimming was another popular sport. In April 1872 the *Bee* reported that Burns Slough, a waterway running parallel to the tracks of the Sacramento Valley Railroad on R Street, was "filled with more naked and unruly small boys than pollywogs."

Many of the people who settled in the Sacramento region brought with them a tradition of concern and caring for their neighbors. As they had done back East and in their homelands, they organized mutual assistance societies. Since many of the new arrivals were natives of Germany, Ireland, and Scotland, they organized ethnic associations along those lines. Men in business and trades organized fraternal associations. Women organized auxiliaries. Such organizations created a lively social atmosphere—with dances, balls, and parties, and provided assistance for any members in need.

Newcomers arrived daily, and many had no such group to turn to. In

The Chinese settled on I Street, along Sutter's Slough, sometimes called China Slough. The Chinese first came to Sacramento during the Gold Rush. Later, the first Chinese settlement was swelled by workers returning from the grueling work on the Central Pacific Railroad. Courtesy, Sacramento City Library Collection, SMHD

1857 a group of Sacramento's leading businessmen organized the Howard Benevolent Society, the sole purpose of which was "the relief of the sick and destitute." Funds came via membership fees, voluntary contributions, and legislative grants. The Lady Howards held sewing bees to make clothing for the poor.

In 1857, the same year that the Howards were organized, a small band of Catholic nuns, the Sisters of Mercy, arrived from San Francisco. They started a school in the basement of the Catholic church at 7th and K, and became the city's first visiting nurses, carrying baskets of food and medicine and words of comfort to the sick.

Another charitable group of women organized and ran the Protestant Orphan Asylum. Beginning in 1867 with a grant from the state and donations from citizens, the Board of Lady Managers rented and furnished a building at 7th and D, hired a matron, and immediately took in a dozen children. The following year the managers bought a block of land at 18th and K and built a permanent home, caring for 50 or more children at a time.

Sacramento's first theater opened in 1849. Located on Front Street next to the saloon, the Eagle Theater was a modest wooden and canvas structure with a tin roof. The miners sat on plank benches facing the raised stage, and ladies sat in a balcony which they reached by an outside ladder.

New York Tribune reporter Bayard Taylor attended the opening night in mid-October 1849, which starred Mrs. Henry Ray of the Royal Theater, New Zealand, in the tragic drama, "The Bandit Chief." He reported:

> *The bell rings, the curtain rolls up, and we look upon a forest scene, in the midst of which appears Hildebrand, the robber, in a sky-blue mantle. Mrs. Ray rushes in and throws herself into an attitude in the middle of the stage; why she does it no one can tell. This movement, which she repeats several times in the course of the first three acts, has no connection with the tragedy; it is evidently introduced for the purpose of showing the audience that there is, actually, a female performer.*
>
> *The miners, to whom the sight of a woman is not a frequent occurrence, are delighted with these passages and applaud vehemently.*

This Lawrence and Houseworth view taken in 1866 shows 7th and K streets, one of the major intersections in Sacramento during the 19th century. The tower of the St. Rose of Lima church dominated the landscape. Built in 1851, the Golden Eagle Hotel stood across the street from the church for over a century. The hotel site is now occupied by Liberty House department store, and the church site is now a city park. Courtesy, Southern Pacific Collection, SMHD

When Sacramento flooded a month later, drama-craving miners sloshed through knee-deep water to the performances. Inside the theater the waters rose to the level of the seats. Actor John McCabe described the antics of the audience:

> *Some of the miners took great pleasure in wading along the seats covered with water and sitting on the railing round the orchestra. On several occasions when the company were 'piling on the agony' in the stage, one of these miners would appear to be roused to enthusiasm, and while shouting his approbation, would throw his arms open, striking his neighbors on each side, and precipitating them backwards into the water.*
>
> *This practical joke sometimes caused a laugh, sometimes a fight, and always interrupted the performance for awhile.*

As the rains continued into January, the Eagle closed. After the floods subsided, it was sold, and the new owners moved it to 2nd Street and renamed it the Tehama. The Tehama burned to the ground in the fire of August 14, 1851, but by this time there were several theaters, and the people of Sacramento were enjoying a variety of forms of dramatic entertainment, including plays, musicals, and concerts.

As the city prospered, art and architecture flourished. Affluent families built elegant homes and furnished them with care. In 1870 Edwin B. Crocker, State Supreme Court judge and chief counsel to the Central Pacific Railroad, traveled through Europe with his wife Margaret collecting paintings, drawings, sculptures, and other masterpieces. When the Crockers returned, they built an art gallery beside their home, with a billiard room, skating rink, and bowling alley in the basement, and invited the citizens of Sacramento to share in the enjoyment of their treasures. In 1872, the *Union* praised the new addition to the city's cultural life:

> *The enterprise of Judge Crocker ought to be hailed as one of the signs of the dawning of an era of sentiment when something more than coins and provender will absorb the minds of our countrymen. Art flourished under Grecian skies, and why not here where all the charms of earth and sky are blended?*

To promote greater interest in the fine arts, David Lubin of the Weinstock-Lubin department store organized the California Museum Associ-

The Charles and Anna Luhrs family took a moment from their croquet game to pose for a family picture at their residence on the northwest corner of 13th and P streets. George D. Stewart took this photograph in 1888. The large wheels of the baby carriage were useful on Sacramento's bumpy and muddy streets. Courtesy, Crocker Art Museum Collection, SMHD

The intersection of 7th and K streets has been a landmark in Sacramento for many years. The imposing sandstone post office building replaced the St. Rose of Lima church in the 1890s. The post office stood until the K Street Mall was redeveloped in the 1960s. The site is now occupied by the St. Rose of Lima Park. Courtesy, California State Library Collection, SMHD

ation in 1884, with the widowed Mrs. Crocker as one of the directors. A leader in charitable and cultural activities, she gave her own gallery and its treasures to the city. To show their gratitude, the citizens held a magnificent Flower Festival in her honor on May 6, 1885.

In a letter to San Francisco newspapers festival planners explained why people who knew her held her in high esteem:

> *A woman of wealth, she has taught the people, in the truest sense, how worldly possessions can be made to adorn a noble character.*

Christian ministers arrived with the '49ers, some to find gold, some to save souls. The Reverend J.A. Benton, who arrived in the summer of 1849, recalled the early development of religion in the community:

> *One of the first sermons was delivered by the Rev. J.W. Douglass sometime in March 1849. In May the Rev. W. Grove Deal instituted a regular preaching service, which was held here and there, according to convenience. It was in the month of September that people began processes of denominational organization. The church edifice of the Congregational Church was built in the autumn of 1850.*

The Reverend Benton preached his first sermon in Sacramento, "the city of tents and trees," on Sunday, July 22, 1849. The congregation of about 100 men and three women gathered in a beautiful grove of oaks, with an ox-wagon serving as the pulpit, and the tongue and yoke providing seating for the choir. A few seats were improvised from crates and planks, but most of the congregation remained standing throughout the hour-long service.

Over the next 30 years, some 20 separate denominational groups were formed. In the early 1850s a Jewish congregation bought the Methodist Episcopal Church on 7th Street and turned it into Sacramento's first synagogue. The Catholic church, St. Rose of Lima, remained a city landmark from the time it was built at 7th and K in 1854 until it was torn down to make room for a new post office in the 1880s. In the 1880s and 1890s, many denominations built elegant churches of brick or stone, featuring stained glass windows, distinctive steeples and impressive bell towers. Under Bishop Patrick Manogue, the Catholic Church began construction on the Cathedral of the Blessed Sacrament, which was completed and dedicated in 1889. An observer described its impressive appearance:

> *The elegant proportions of the structure, its majestic dome rising to a height of over two hundred feet, its classic arches and arched ceiling set in frames of varied frescoes, the harmony of due proportions in dimensions, the storied windows, rare paintings and the statuary it contains, endear both the structure and its venerable builder to Sacramento citizens, irrespective of creed or class.*

With its churches, schools, and cultural events, Sacramento by the 1890s took great pride in its progress from its rough-and-tumble Gold Rush beginnings. Substantial brick and stone churches and schools provided external evidence of the people's aspirations for intellectual, cultural, and spiritual growth. While rising above physical adversity, the people sought the higher life of mind and spirit.

The Cathedral of the Blessed Sacrament was constructed at 11th and K streets during the late 1880s. This church replaced the St. Rose of Lima church that was at 7th and K streets. For years the cathedral marked the east end of the K Street business district. The Cathedral of the Blessed Sacrament is still functioning today and is undergoing restoration. Courtesy, California State Library Collection, SMHD

This turn of the century photograph was taken from the top of the State Capitol, looking northwest. The intersection of 10th and L streets is at the lower right. Sacramento landmarks, the Golden Eagle Hotel and the Sacramento Post Office at the intersection of 7th and K streets, can be seen at the middle of the photograph. By this time many of the downtown streets had been paved. Courtesy, J. Walzer Collection, SMHD

Chapter 4

REDEEMED AND REGENERATED
1850-1880

Even while struggling for survival, first-generation Sacramentans set about to secure political and economic power. They made their city the state capital, the site of the annual state fair, and the terminus of the transcontinental railroad. The railroad brought Sacramento into the mainstream of economic and cultural development, completing the changeover from frontier outpost to burgeoning city.

The Sacramentans who secured the state capital in 1854 made their city the center of political power in the West. Even while establishing their fledgling city, Sacramentans helped set up the state government in 1849—and they did it without assistance from the federal government. Although the United States claimed California as its territory in 1846, the Congresses of 1846, 1847, and 1848 failed to set up a territorial government. In 1849, after Congress met and adjourned, again without giving California any kind of official standing, the military governor, General Bennett Riley, called for a constitutional convention.

In mid-summer of 1849, California voters elected delegates to organize their new state. John Sutter and several Sacramentans were among those elected to go to the convention in Monterey, the traditional capital of Alta California. From September 1 to October 12, 48 delegates hammered out a document modeled after the U.S. Constitution: it outlined the rights of citizens and established a two-house legislature, the position of governor, and a system of courts. The new document was completed on October 13, and, following a 31-gun salute symbolizing California's hoped-for admission as the 31st state, John Sutter (with typical military formality) presented the constitution to General Riley.

One month later, on November 13, California voters ratified the document and elected a governor and representatives to the state legislature. Judge Peter Burnett, who had helped sell Sacramento's first lots, won out over Sutter and two others and became the first governor of California. Another Sacramentan, John McDougal, became lieutenant governor. (McDougal became governor a year later, when Burnett resigned.) John Bidwell, Sutter's right-hand man since 1841, was elected to the state senate.

Because representation in the state legislature was apportioned by population, 25 percent of the seats—four in the senate and nine in the assembly—went to Sacramento. Another 25 percent went to the adjacent mining region of San Joaquin, leaving just half of the seats for all the rest of the state.

The first legislature convened in the little pueblo town of San Jose on December 17, 1849. The assembly met on the second floor of an unfinished, two-story adobe hotel; the senate met in a private home nearby. Legislators complained about the lack of accommodations during that cold and rainy winter. General Mariano Vallejo offered his property for the capital, promising to build a city and give the state 156 acres, and in October 1850 the people voted to accept his proposal. But since Vallejo was unable to get any buildings ready in time for the meeting of the legislature three months later, the lawmakers met again in San Jose, opening the second session on January 6, 1851. By this time California was officially a state, having been admitted to the Union on September 9, 1850.

Upon arriving in Vallejo the following year, the elected representatives found only one building completed, with no furniture, and few places to eat or sleep. They took a vote, and that afternoon caught a steamboat for Sacramento. Although they arrived at 3 a.m., the levee was crowded with people, cheering and firing a cannon to welcome them.

Sacramento offered everything the legislators could desire: a meeting place (the recently-built county courthouse), hotels, restaurants, laundries, transportation, and entertainment. Nevertheless, it was still only the temporary capital. Due to the fire of November 2, 1852, which was followed a little more than a month later by a flood, Sacramento was in no condition to receive the legislature of 1853. The lawmakers reconvened in Vallejo, as planned, but found little improvement over the past 12 months. They then moved to nearby Benicia on February 11, 1853.

Facing page: The California State Capitol was completed in 1874. This 1879 photograph shows the formally landscaped grounds. Several of the Italian stone pines and the deodor cedars inside the fence still stand today. Courtesy, Lucinda M. Woodward

Located on 2nd Street, the Arcade was one of Sacramento's prominent hotels during the 19th century. The state capital's presence in Sacramento increased the business of the local hotels and restaurants and conferred a general economic benefit to the city. Other prominent hotels included the Orleans, Western, Golden Eagle, and the Senator. Courtesy, Sacramento Housing and Redevelopment Agency Collection, SMHD

Although unable to host the legislature that year, Sacramento citizens rolled up their sleeves, cleaned up the ashes and mud, and built anew. After the fire, ex-governor Peter Burnett, who had retired to Alviso, returned to Sacramento to run for city council and help in the rebuilding. At his instigation the city laid heavy wooden planks along J Street from the levee out to the city limits, making it passable year-round. Surveying the progress of the work, Burnett announced to a friend, "We shall have the prettiest city in the state, and stand redeemed and regenerated!"

The fifth legislature convened again in Benicia on January 2, 1854, and scheduled another vote on the permanent location of the capital. Sacramento lobbyists were at work even before the lawmakers arrived. According to some sources, a delegation of some 200 to 300 Sacramentans went to Benicia ahead of time and reserved all the hotel rooms and lodgings so that legislators had to sleep in state offices, taverns, and even stables. The city of Sacramento offered the legislature the use of their courthouse, a free lot for the building of a state capitol, and a fireproof vault for the archives. Local newspapers offered facilities for printing the minutes and other state documents. To gain the support of the Nevada County delegation, Peter Burnett secured a petition from more than 500 Nevada County voters, which was published in the *Sacramento Union*. In another tactic, the Sacramento legislators agreed to support San Franciscan David Broderick's candidacy for the U.S. Senate in return for his delegation's vote for Sacramento as the capital. The city's zealous actions worked: the legislature passed the bill to move to Sacramento, and it became law February 25, when it was signed by Governor John Bigler, another Sacramentan.

The lawmakers promptly packed their bags and loaded their furniture onto the *Wilson G. Hunt*, which had been chartered by the city of Sacramento, and steamed up the river to the new capital. The *Sacramento Union* described the welcome given the legislature on the morning of February 26, 1854:

The major hotels provided transportation for their guests from the steamer landing and the railroad station to their establishments. The Western Hotel was purchased by William Land and became one of Sacramento's best-known hotels. Courtesy, Sacramento City Library Collection, SMHD

From the moment the gallant steamer hoved in sight, 'til her prow touched the landing, a discharge of cannon was kept up at regular intervals, intermingled with the shouts of an immense multitude of people, who had assembled on the levee to witness the spectacle and give eclat to the joyful occasion. The Sutter Rifles, in their gayest uniforms and with a superior band of music, were also on the ground, and formed the vanguard of a procession which escorted his excellency, the governor, and other dignitaries to the Orleans Hotel. There speeches were made, rifles fired, and the crowds cheered in welcome.

The state capitol was under construction between 1860 and 1874. This view of the east side, taken about 1868, shows the brick construction technique, the incomplete dome, and an apse that was removed after World War II to make room for the East Annex. Courtesy, California Department of Parks and Recreation Collection, SMHD

The rest of the 1854 session was held in the courthouse. That summer fire struck the city once again, and on July 13 the courthouse burned down. The citizens of Sacramento wasted no time. They placed a cornerstone for a new and larger courthouse on September 27. By January, just in time for the next session, the two-story Grecian style building was completed. Its broad portico was supported by eight fluted pillars. It was large enough for both the senate and assembly chambers and the other offices of the state.

In 1856 the legislature voted $300,000 in bonds to build a capitol on the block bounded by 9th, 10th, I, and J streets, which had been given to the state by the city. When the Supreme Court decided that this bond issue would increase the state debt beyond its legal limits, the project was postponed and the block reverted to the city. This was one of the blocks designated by John Sutter, Jr., for a public park, and the city landscaped it and named it Plaza Park. Later Sacramentans gave the state a new and larger site—the four blocks bounded by 10th, 12th, L, and N streets.

Ground was broken for the new capitol building on September 24, 1860, and the following May a crowd of about 3,000 gathered for the ceremonial placement of the cornerstone. The work was interrupted in its early stages by the floods of the winter of 1861-1862. Because the courthouse was also flooded, the legislature moved temporarily to San Francisco. Undismayed by the devastation, the *Sacramento Union* asserted that the city would quickly

Above: Quarrying for granite to be used in the capitol building began at Folsom, but the granite was too coarse. Quarrying shifted in 1864 to a site on the Central Pacific line near Rocklin. This photo was taken by Alfred Hart in the late 1860s. Courtesy, Southern Pacific Company Collection, SMHD

Above right: Hauling the iron columns for the state capitol through the streets of Sacramento from the waterfront was a tremendous task. The columns were pulled by Oliver Hyde's patent American Overland Steamer. This photograph was taken near 3rd and J streets in May 1871. Courtesy, Higgins Collection, University of California, Davis and California State Capitol Museum

recover: "Like the Phoenix she has sprung from the ashes of her past ruin, and beautiful as Venus she will now arise from the waves."

The early years of construction were plagued by material shortages and cost overruns. Yet the builders persevered. Governor Leland Stanford, in his annual message in 1863, affirmed, "The State Capitol of California, that is to endure for generations, should be a structure that the future will be proud of, and surrounded with a beauty and luxuriousness that no other capitol in the country could boast."

Late in 1869 the capitol, although not yet completed, was opened for use. The senate and assembly met in their new chambers, and the governor and secretary of state occupied their new offices. On December 15 leading dignitaries and their elegantly attired ladies attended a grand ball in the chambers, lit by hundreds of newly-installed gas burners.

The capitol was officially declared completed in 1874.

Although the local papers were staunch supporters of Sacramento's status as state capital, they did not relinquish their traditional role as critics of the political process. Upon the adjournment of the 1872 legislature, the *Union* commented wryly: "The dome of the Capitol was illuminated last night, probably as a demonstration of rejoicing over the close of the session."

The *Bee* in 1893 nearly pushed the legislature into the waiting arms of San Jose, one of many cities that had been lobbying for the capital over the years. Its front page on Saturday, March 11, bore the headline:

THANK GOD THE SESSION NOW IS ALMOST OVER

Some of the legislators took offense at the *Bee's* charges of corruption, and rushed a bill through both houses that evening to have Californians vote to move the capital to San Jose. When merchants and citizens heard the news the next day they reacted with disbelief, dismay, and panic. They held a public meeting at the courthouse, denounced the *Bee's* words, and passed a resolution assuring the legislature that "the *Bee* in no way represented the sentiments of the community."

The Board of Trade (forerunner of the chamber of commerce) ordered a boycott against the *Bee*. Publisher C.K. McClatchy countered that the *Bee's* charges were true and it would be happy to prove them.

"The question naturally excited attention all over the United States," the *Bee* later recalled. "On the Coast particularly it was discussed and made the occasion for many a joke at the expense of Sacramento, to the effect that she was a silurian town without enterprise, and would disappear from the map if she lost the capital."

Smarting from the embarrassment, Sacramentans pitched in to prove their progressiveness. Despite the financial depression of 1893, the city paved its main streets with asphalt, replaced rough board sidewalks with smooth concrete, built several miles of electric street railway, raised funds to bring in new manufacturing industries, designed a modern sewage system, and voted bonds for a new supply of clear water.

A year later the *Bee* reported that the city's efforts "commanded universal admiration, and gave Sacramento a prestige which she can never lose save through her own fault."

The question was put to the test in 1908, when the city of Berkeley's bid for the capital was put on the ballot. The state's voters turned down Berkeley's proposal by a margin of two to one.

Early Sacramentans went after the state fair with the same zeal with which they had secured the capital. They had organized an agricultural fair in 1852, then persuaded the legislature to set up the State Agricultural Society,

In 1903 the legislature purchased the Steffens/Gallatin mansion at 16th and H streets for use as a governor's mansion. Governor Pardee and his family occupied the house that year. This was the first state-owned governor's mansion. Built in 1877, the house was continuously used as a residence until the 1960s when Governor Reagan chose to live elsewhere. The site is now operated by the California Department of Parks and Recreation. Courtesy, Sacramento Housing and Redevelopment Agency Collection, SMHD

which sponsored the first state fair in San Francisco in 1854. Sacramento hosted the fair in 1855, followed in the next three years by San Jose, Stockton, and Marysville. In preparation for the fair's return in 1859, Sacramentans bought a block of land at 6th and M which they gave to the society. They then raised funds to match a state grant for an exhibit hall or pavilion at the site. They also leased a two-block area, bounded by 11th, 12th, O, and Q streets, for livestock displays.

Sacramento once again secured the state fair in 1860—to others' chagrin. A San Francisco newspaper accused Sacramento citizens of joining the Agricultural Society solely to vote on the issue of the state fair site, but defenders answered that if Sacramento was so interested as to provide 800 of the 1,200 members, she was entitled to the site. Sacramentans reinforced their bid by buying a 20-acre livestock site in the blocks bounded by 20th, 22nd, E, and H streets, where they built a race track and grandstand. They donated the new facility, Agricultural Park, to the society. By an overwhelming majority, the society voted to make Sacramento the fair's permanent home.

Geologist William Brewer, who visited Sacramento at fair time in 1861, described the scene at Agricultural Park:

The second California State Fair was held in Sacramento in September 1855. That year the livestock show and races were held at the Louisiana Racetrack near the intersection of 12th Avenue and Franklin Boulevard. Courtesy, California State Library Collection, SMHD

The Fair is like other fairs—hundreds of big cattle, horses, etc. (the horses the finest), some few sheep, fewer hogs, some mules and jacks. The grounds are fine, over 20 acres enclosed with a high brick wall with ten entrances. The stalls for cattle are finely arranged around the outside. There is a large stand for two thousand spectators, and a fine track. The races were received with California gusto, where horsemanship is such an accomplishment.

By now agriculture was thoroughly established as the basis for California's economy, and Sacramento County led the state in the production of apples, peaches, plums, quinces, lemons, olives, pomegranates, almonds, walnuts, and raspberries.

In the early 1880s the city and county again raised money to match state funds for a new and larger site. While continuing to use Agricultural Park for livestock exhibits and horse racing, the fair sponsors built a new pavilion at the capitol grounds in time for the fair of 1884.

When the state took over the management of the fair in 1904, the Agricultural Society sold the park and bought 100 acres to the southeast of the city, which it deeded to the state. Three years later the old pavilion in Capitol

Park was torn down and a new one built at Stockton and Broadway. More acreage was added, and in 1909 for the first time all parts of the fair—exhibits, entertainment, livestock, and racing—were together on the same site, where they remained for over half a century.

Besides being the major social event of the year, the state fair reinforced Sacramento's primacy as the economic and political center of the state. It attracted thousands of people annually, providing a showcase for the state's economic backbone, agriculture, and put Sacramento's farming techniques, homemaking skills, labor-saving devices, inventions, and new technologies in the forefront.

While Sacramentans were consolidating their position as a political and economic power center within the new state of California, they were also reaching back toward the main body of civilization in the states on the Eastern seaboard. They did this by building transcontinental communications and transportation systems to carry news, people, and freight.

Sacramento permanently captured the state fair in 1861. In 1883 the city and county of Sacramento raised money for a new state fair pavilion. From 1884 to 1905 the new pavilion stood near the corner of 15th and N streets in Capitol Park, replacing an earlier pavilion at 6th and M streets. The new building housed exhibits while the horse races took place between B, H, 26th, and 22nd streets. In 1905 the state fair moved again to a site on Stockton Boulevard and Broadway. Courtesy, Crocker Art Museum Collection, SMHD

Disaster as entertainment has persevered throughout history. After the grandstand was completed at the state fair site on Stockton Boulevard, staged locomotive collisions became a popular feature for fairgoers. This event was staged in September 1916. Courtesy, California State Library Collection, SMHD

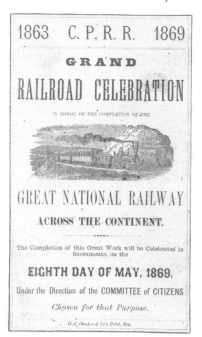

Top: Sacramentans planned a parade to celebrate the completion of the transcontinental railroad in May 1869. Expecting that the railroad would be completed on May 8, they printed the parade program with that date. The Central and Union Pacific lines met two days later, so the parade was delayed accordingly. Courtesy, Norman L. Wilson

Above: During the second half of the 19th century, stages, trains, and boats all converged at Sacramento. Although the stagelines were more widespread before the railroad, they continued to serve the areas not reached by the iron ribbons. Courtesy, Sacramento Museum and History Division Collecton, SMHD

In May 1869, just 20 years after the Gold Rush, Sacramento and the nation prepared to celebrate the completion of the railroad that would link California to the Eastern states. The first shovelful of dirt unearthed to make way for the railroad had been removed from the foot of K Street six years earlier by Governor Leland Stanford, one of four Sacramento merchants who backed the ambitious project. While the Central Pacific pushed its rails from Sacramento to the east through the Sierras, across Nevada, and into the desert of Utah, the Union Pacific built westward from Omaha. The two lines of track were scheduled to meet at Promontory Point, Utah, on Saturday, May 8.

The day before, Stanford had wired from Promontory Point that the Union Pacific wasn't ready, for the car carrying the top Union Pacific officials had been captured and held hostage by some 400 railroad workers who had not been paid since January. The workers were subsequently paid and the officials were released on Friday, but the last section of track wouldn't be completed until Monday.

Nonetheless, Sacramento went ahead with its celebration. Well-wishers from all around the state began arriving at the passenger station on Front Street Saturday at 5 a.m. The *Union* reported, "By 9 o'clock the city was crowded in all the principal streets with the largest, most orderly, and eager number of people ever collected here at one time—and still they came, from farms, roads, river, in boats, cars, and every conceivable style of conveyance, till the sidewalks were too small to hold the throng."

The signal for rejoicing was given at 10 a.m. by a shot from the Union Boy, the cannon which had announced the news of each Northern victory during the Civil War. Simultaneously 23 locomotives at the levee blasted their whistles, and for 15 minutes every bell in the city rang out. Citizens formed in units for a grand parade, followed by speeches, banquets, and toasts. The *Sacramento Union* asserted proudly, "The victory of today—a continent crossed—assures us that henceforth roads and telegraphs are to be the pioneers of progress."

Shortly after noon on Monday, May 10, 1869, the telegraph office on Front Street received word that the last spike had been hammered home.

Sacramento's jubilation was unbounded, for the trail that led from the Gold Rush to the Golden Spike had been 20 years in the making. The Golden Spike represented the culmination of the efforts of transplanted Easterners to reconnect with their Eastern origins; aggressive, perserving pioneers seized upon each new technological advance to speed the movement of news, people, and freight. The cross-country trip that had taken six months in 1849 now could be made in six days.

Among important milestones, Sacramento, as early as 1853, had become the telegraphic hub of Northern California, with two companies enabling news to travel between telegraph points almost instantaneously. The California State Telegraph connected Sacramento to San Francisco, San Jose, and Marysville, while the wires of the Alta California Telegraph served the mountain mining areas.

Meanwhile stagecoaches speeded the mail service. In 1858 two Eastern businessmen, John Butterfield and William Fargo, organized the Great Overland Mail Company. The stage route linked San Francisco to Missouri and Tennessee, and cut to three weeks the time for letters and express mail between East and West. Two years later three Kansas City freight line operators set up a competing service which cut that time in half—the Pony Express. The Alta California Telegraph became the Sacramento agent and Western terminus for the new stage line.

For 18 months the ponies carried mail between Sacramento and St. Joseph, Missouri, a distance of nearly 2,000 miles, averaging ten days' time each way. When the South seceded from the Union early in 1861, the Pony Express brought the news to Sacramento. It brought the text of President Abraham Lincoln's inaugural speech in March, and in April it brought the news of the South's attack on Fort Sumter—the first shots of the Civil War.

As the transcontinental telegraph neared completion in the fall of 1861, the financially troubled Pony Express ceased operations, ending a legendary chapter in the annals of the West. The telegraph was cheaper and faster.

The outbreak of war in 1861 paved the way for the transcontinental railroad. Such a road had been debated in Congress for two decades, but Northern and Southern representatives had deadlocked over a choice of routes. After the South seceded, however, the federal government sought the overland link with California as a military measure for the transportation of troops and mails. On July 1, 1862, President Lincoln signed the Pacific Railroad Act delegating the Union Pacific to build westward from Omaha, Nebraska, while the Central Pacific would build eastward from Sacramento.

Sacramentans had been planning for such a railroad for about 20 years. As early as 1852 the state's first governor, Peter Burnett, and several others attempted to promote a railroad along the Sierra foothills to Marysville, but attempts to secure sufficient funding failed. Two years later another group organized the Sacramento Valley Railroad company. One of the members went back to New York in search of financial backing and returned with a young engineer, Theodore Judah, who had recently built a railroad over the Niagara Gorge.

Freighting to the mountains was a highly profitable business in the 1850s. Typically, a team of six or eight mules pulled a California wagon loaded with about three to four tons of goods. To estimate the potential market for the railroad, Judah stationed himself near Sutter's Fort, counting the teams which passed daily. He calculated about 700 teams making one round trip a week during the trading season, bearing a total of 70,000 tons of goods in a year.

Ground was broken for the Sacramento Valley Railroad at 3rd and R on February 12, 1855, and tracks were laid along the R Street levee heading east. Twelve months later the road reached 22 miles to Folsom. It proved its usefulness in carrying tons of cobblestones—"Folsom potatoes"—and granite from Folsom-area quarries for streets and buildings in Sacramento and San Fran-

Theodore Judah was a civil engineer who came to Sacramento in 1854. He engineered the Sacramento Valley Railroad and selected the route for the Central Pacific Railroad. He died in 1863 at the age of 37 after contracting yellow fever in Panama on his way east to attract backers for the transcontinental railroad project. Courtesy, Southern Pacific Company Collection, SMHD

The trial run of the Sacramento Valley Railroad, which connected Sacramento with Folsom, was made on August 17, 1855. This illustration of the event appeared in the January 1, 1856 edition of the *Pictorial Union.* Courtesy, Southern Pacific Company Collection, SMHD

Four powerful Sacramentans formed the Central Pacific Railroad Company in 1861. The group, called "The Big Four," included: (left to right) newly-elected California Governor Leland Stanford; state senator and retailer Charles Crocker; and the mercantile team of Collis P. Huntington and Mark Hopkins. The railroad turned these men into American barons. From Circker, *Dictionary of American Portraits,* Dover, 1967

Central Pacific master mechanic Andrew J. Stevens spent his life designing railroad equipment. He designed this locomotive using many of his favorite features. The locomotive rolled out of the Sacramento shops in 1882 and saw over 50 years of service. A statue of Stevens, paid for by Central Pacific employees, now stands in City Plaza. Courtesy, *Recent Locomotives,* 1883, reprinted in *Early American Locomotives,* Dover, 1972

cisco. After the Comstock Lode was discovered in Nevada in 1859, the railroad began to turn a profit. Goods from San Francisco came up the Sacramento River to the levee, where they were transferred to the railroad for the leg to Folsom. There they were loaded onto freight wagons headed for Virginia City. Silver from the Nevada mines was shipped by wagon to Folsom, then by railroad to Sacramento and by steamer to San Francisco.

Since the city council represented competing interests, it passed regulations which increased road construction and maintenance costs, and levied taxes on goods transferred from boats to the train. When the American River overflowed in December 1861, the R Street levee had trapped the floodwaters in the city. Blaming the Sacramento Valley Railroad for the damages, city officials, a year later, ordered the tracks torn up between 6th Street and the waterfront. Goods to be transferred from boats to the train then had to be hauled by wagon teams six blocks to make the connection.

As a countermove, the railroad's San Francisco stockholders voted to build a branch line from Brighton Station to a point on the river nine miles south of the embarcadero. Since goods loaded onto the railroad there would not be subject to city taxes, they named the spot Freeport. Investors built the 10-mile Freeport Railroad line in the fall and winter of 1863, then leased it to the Sacramento Valley Railroad.

After the road had reached Folsom in 1856, its chief engineer, Theodore

Judah, turned his interest to the Sierras, spending his summers walking the trails and talking to seasoned pioneers. A dentist in the little town of Dutch Flat pointed him toward Emigrant Gap and Donner Pass. After investigating the route in 1860, Judah returned to seek financing for a rail line through the high Sierras. Bankers in San Francisco shook their heads, calling him "crazy Judah," and turned him down. Sacramento financiers were equally skeptical, but Judah's proposal did capture the imagination of a successful wholesale grocer, Leland Stanford, who gathered a group of friends to listen. Among them were Charles Crocker, a dry goods merchant, and Collis P. Huntington and Mark Hopkins, owners of Huntington & Hopkins hardware store. The four merchants and Judah incorporated the Central Pacific Railroad on June 28, 1861.

While Judah solved the enormous engineering problems involved in building a railroad through the steep, rocky mountain passes, the four businessmen answered the financial and political challenges. While Judah went back to Washington to lobby Congress, Leland Stanford won California's governorship. After taking office in January 1862, he persuaded the legislature to grant subsidies to the railroad project and appointed the Central Pacific's chief legal counsel, Edwin B. Crocker (Charles' brother), to the State Supreme Court.

Hundreds of citizens turned out for groundbreaking ceremonies at Front and K on January 8, 1863. Addressing the crowd, Governor Stanford envisioned the day "when the Pacific will be bound to the Atlantic by iron bonds, that shall consolidate and strengthen the ties of nationality, and advance with giant strides the prosperity of the State and of our country."

A year later the iron rails extended only 18 miles (to Roseville). The war between the states made building materials scarce and expensive. Judah, meanwhile, had broken with his partners over policy questions in October and left for New York. He died shortly after arriving on the East Coast, having contracted yellow fever while crossing the Isthmus of Panama.

Charles Crocker's Sacramento residence was located at the corner of 8th and F streets in the area known today as Alkalai Flat. The building was later used as a Southern Pacific hospital. Crocker was one of the Central Pacific "Big Four." Courtesy, Southern Pacific Company Collection, SMHD

The Huntington and Hopkins hardware store at 54 K Street was a landmark known around the world. Charles Crocker, C.P. Huntington, Mark Hopkins, and Leland Stanford, four Sacramento merchants, planned the Central Pacific Railroad in the store's upstairs room. This view, showing employees and merchandise from the store, was taken in the late 1860s. Courtesy, California State Library Collection, SMHD

In 1869 this railroad bridge across the Sacramento River was built at I Street by the California Pacific Railroad Company, replacing an earlier wagon bridge. The Central Pacific Depot, built in 1879, can be seen at the east end of the bridge. Courtesy, Sacramento City Library Collection, SMHD

By May 1865, the road reached 36 miles to Auburn. As tracklaying advanced into the mountains, workers left in droves to go prospecting. Charles Crocker, in charge of construction, suggested trying Chinese workers, but Superintendent J.H. Strobridge scoffed at the idea, arguing that the Orientals were too lightweight to lift heavy ties. Crocker replied that one working alone perhaps was, but two or more teamed together could do anything—after all, they built the Great Wall of China.

Crocker brought in the first crew of 50 Chinese laborers in 1865, and the results were phenomenal. Soon railroad agents were recruiting thousands of Chinese, not only from California, but from South China as well. At the peak of construction, the Central Pacific employed more than 10,000 Chinese.

The first Chinese in California—two men and a woman—had arrived in 1848. The Gold Rush attracted thousands more. Many of the immigrants from the Celestial Empire settled in Sacramento along the I Street shoreline of Sutter Slough. Keeping their native language and customs, many started grocery stores and laundries, while some found employment as domestic servants.

The Chinese constituted a community within a community, publishing

The Central Pacific roundhouse was featured in this Johnson Brothers photograph. The roundhouse was one of the original brick buildings built at the railroad shops near Sutter's Slough. By the 1950s the newer, longer locomotives were no longer able to use this structure, and so it was demolished. Courtesy, California State Library Collection, SMHD

their own newspaper in the 1850s. In September 1854 two rival tongs—Chinese secret societies—got into a pitched battle on I Street. About 500 Chinese fought each other with spears and tridents.

When they went to work on the railroad, Chinese workers persevered long after other workers gave up. They moved enormous quantities of earth with wheelbarrows and one-horse dump carts to fill in deep gaps. They chiseled roadways out of solid granite. At one point they were suspended in wicker baskets on the face of a granite cliff while they hammered and chiseled at the rock.

As the city celebrated the completion of the task in 1869, Judge Edwin B. Crocker paid the following tribute to the Chinese:

Fellow citizens, we have met to celebrate the completion of one of the greatest works of the age, and in the midst of our rejoicing at this event I wish to call to your minds that the early completion of the railroad we have built has been in a great measure due to that poor, despised class of laborers called the Chinese—to the fidelity and industry they have shown, and the great amount of laborers of this land that have been employed upon this work.

The first full load of deciduous fruit left Sacramento for the East on June 24, 1886. The ability to transport fresh produce revolutionized the agricultural economy around Sacramento. Tandem engines helped the trains climb the Sierra grades. Courtesy, Southern Pacific Company Collection, SMHD

The coming of the railroad had a profound impact on all aspects of life in the Sacramento area, as people, freight, and mails moved across the continent with greater ease than ever before. At the time of the celebration the *Union* philosophized, "The shuttle certainly moves faster in the web of time, and whether or not it yield us product of hand or brain finer in quality than those of Rome, Greek, or Assyrian, we may be sure the quantity will be far greater and more evenly distributed."

Chapter 5
DAWN OF A NEW CENTURY
1880-1930

After securing political and economic power, Sacramentans turned their attention to harnessing nature's power. They brought hydroelectric power into the city, and formed companies to market new inventions such as the telephone. The automobile brought a permanent transformation in city life, with World War I providing a convenient line of demarkation between horse-and-buggy days and modernization.

Sacramentans celebrated Admission Day in 1895 by lighting up the city as never before. Electric power generated from a spot on the American River 22 miles away dazzled old-timers and newcomers alike.

"Sacramento's pulse beat high and fast last night," reported the *Bee* on the day after the Carnival of Lights. "She had cast aside the old and faded robes of her humble childhood days and stood at the new altar of celestial fire to be made the bride of Progress of the new century that is about to dawn."

Up till the summer of 1895, electricity had been generated by batteries or steam. It was used primarily for instruments that required little power—the telegraph, burglar alarms, stable bells. But the new hydroelectric plant at Folsom gave Sacramento a source of cheap and abundant energy for light, heat, factories, and transportation. The *Bee* reported:

> Not only is this the longest power transmission in the world, but it is also the largest electric power plant in the world, in the sense of the power actually developed . . . with a capacity of 4,000 horse power actually delivered for use in this city.

Although the establishment of the Folsom plant marked a great advance in city services, public utilities such as the telephone, electric companies, and electric railways had been introduced in embryonic form well before the advent of hydroelectric power. After Alexander Graham Bell invented the telephone in 1876, Sacramentans started experimenting with the new device. In 1878 the American Speaking Telephone Company installed two Bell telephones, one in the Carriage Manufacture Company and one in the Music Parlor. A little later it hooked up a telephone to the telegraph wires so that citizens could talk to San Francisco. One listener said the voices at the other end of the line sounded "as if they proceeded from the bottom of a deep well."

By the summer of 1878, Sacramento newspapers carried advertisements for the telephone, informing readers that "you use it like a speaking tube." Since there was no central exchange, business people strung lines from their offices and homes to the Western Union telegraph office, where a messenger boy would receive the message and deliver it any place in the city for 25 cents. A livery stable owner strung his own line to the telegraph office so that he could dispatch carriages immediately on demand; a doctor connected both his home and office to Western Union for emergency calls; and the city ran a line from the police department to the telegraph office.

In February 1879 J.G. Gill, an electrical engineer, and J.W. Dayton, manager of the Sacramento Mills Company, constructed Sacramento's first continuous telephone line. It was a five-mile-long circuit strung over houses and through trees, connecting 29 businesses with their central switchboard in the telegraph office.

When Gill became the agent for Bell's telephones in 1880, he organized the Sacramento Telephonic Exchange, operating from his electrical store on J Street. A year later he sold out to Bell Telephone, which established the Sacramento District Telegraph Company. Two years later the company became the Sunset Telephone and Telegraph Company.

In 1895, after Bell's patent rights expired, a competing company, Capitol Telephone and Telegraph, offered a second line. Beginning with 300 subscribers, it grew to 1,400 by its fifth year. At first Sacramento residents, expecting cheaper rates, welcomed the competition, but they soon realized there was a severe drawback. Since there was no interchange of communication be-

Facing page: Power lines transmitting electricity long distance from Folsom to Sacramento line this rural section of the Folsom Road. The roadbed of the old Sacramento Valley Railroad parallels the road to the left of the photograph. Armies of power poles marched across the land with the advent of widespread electrification. Courtesy, Ralph Shaw Collection, SMHD

In 1879 the Central Pacific Company constructed this gothic edifice to replace the depot on Front Street. This view shows two eastbound trains. The offices and passenger areas are at the left. Courtesy, Southern Pacific Company Collection, SMHD

tween the two companies, subscribers to one system could not call friends or customers who subscribed to the other. The two companies merged in 1902. Another merger, in 1906, resulted in the Pacific Telephone and Telegraph Company.

In 1879, the same year Gill built Sacramento's first telephone line, electrical wires also made an appearance. *The Sacramento Union* and the Weinstock-Lubin department store co-sponsored the valley's first public display of electric lighting during state fair week, to the amazement of about 5,000 visitors. The newspaper's steam press generated electricity, which was carried by wire over rooftops to light up a set of experimental arc lights in the store display windows.

The hot, smokey arc lights burned with a hissing noise, but were much brighter than the gas lamps which had served the city as the primary source of outdoor illumination for more than a decade. In 1866 the city had installed 45 gas lamps along its main streets and hired a lamplighter, whose job was to light each street lamp at dusk and turn it off later in the evening.

The coming of electricity meant competition for the gas company and a dilemma for the mayor. In 1884 two newly-formed gas companies asked for a city franchise to start an electrical service. The mayor, manager of the gas company, opposed the project as "a humbug piece of business," but the city council voted to allow the erection of poles and wires. Both companies put up their lights on J and K streets on March 29. That summer they brightened up the evening concerts outdoors at the City Plaza.

Incandescent lights, which burned with less heat, smoke, and glare than arc lights, were introduced to Sacramento along J Street shop windows in August 1890. When the cornerstone was laid for the new Weinstock, Lubin & Company department store in 1891, officials expressed pride in the city's progress and confidence in a bright future:

Even the most unimaginative minds must feel that the future advancement will have for its chief factor electricity. We have our store illuminated by electric lights ... The people of this age can boast of electric cars which are as yet very crude in comparison with those of fifty years from today. Then it will be electricity on all sides: in our homes, in business houses, on the streets. As available as the air we breathe, will this subtle fluid meet us and minister to our wants and comforts.

In 1892 the chandeliers and candelabras were removed from the state capitol building to be modified so that they could use either gas or electricity, and outlets were provided for 1,400 incandescent lights. The new interior lighting system was turned on for the public on New Year's Day, 1893.

Electricity was used primarily for illumination rather than power until 1895 because importing the coal needed to generate steam to run the dynamos was so expensive. Despite the cost, by 1890 many manufacturers, including the Southern Pacific shops, had converted to electricity to run their plants.

In the 1880s, a number of hydraulic mining companies experimented with hydroelectric power in the Mother Lode country. The principals of the Natoma Water and Mining Company, Horatio G. Livermore and his two sons, Horatio P. and Charles, formed the Folsom Water Power Company to build a hydroelectric plant at the site of their dam at Folsom. In 1891 the Livermores were joined by Albert Gallatin, general manager of the Huntington and Hopkins Hardware Store, who persuaded others to invest in the powerhouse.

Before beginning work the Livermores incorporated the Sacramento Electric Power and Light Company and obtained a franchise to build an electric streetcar system. Work on the powerhouse started on October 10, 1894. At 4 a.m. on July 13, 1895, the sound of a 100-gun salute roused Sacramento citizens, announcing the successful transmission of power from Folsom Lake to Sacramento.

The Folsom plant enabled Sacramento to celebrate Admission Day—

Sacramento was serviced by a number of telephone companies after the utility was introduced to the city in the late 1870s. The Capital Telephone and Telegraph Company was among the companies acquired by Pacific Telephone and Telegraph in 1906. Despite the claims of this advertisement for long distance calls from Sacramento, a look at the communities which could be reached reveals that none were more than 50 miles away. True transcontinental long distance telephoning was not accomplished until 1915. Courtesy, McClatchy Collection, SMHD

Beginning in 1895, electrical power was generated in this powerhouse near Folsom Dam. This hydroelectric plant provided inexpensive power for the growing city of Sacramento 22 miles away. The economy of Sacramento benefitted from the ready availability of electrical power. The Folsom powerhouse operated until the 1950s when it was replaced by the present Folsom Dam. The powerhouse is now owned by the California Department of Parks and Recreation who operate it as a point of historical interest. Courtesy, California State Library Collection, SMHD

Power generated at Folsom Dam was relayed to this transformer room in Station A at 6th and H in Sacramento. From here the electricity was distributed to Sacramento's households and businesses. Courtesy, Pacific Gas and Electric Company Collection, SMHD

September 9, 1895—with the magnificent Carnival of Lights. The *Bee* reported that over 60,000 people came from all around the valley to witness the spectacle:

> *Twenty-five thousand incandescent lamps, in the cherry red, apple green and orange tints of the carnival made the streets and upper air ablaze with light. They were arranged as maypole streamers on the flag pole at the plaza; they showed from behind and above and below the carnival bunting that clothed the buildings; they illuminated and glorified the beautiful floats in the procession. They outlined the cornices, the roof, and every column, balcony and rib of the great dome of the Capitol building up to the bird cage at the top.*

The Folsom plant also provided power to run streetcars. Battery-operated cars had been tried earlier, but proved unsuccessful because of their limited power. Horse-drawn streetcars had been running since 1861, following a set of rails between the waterfront and the capitol area, and since most homes in the city were within a few blocks of existing streetcar lines, the new electric cars made public transportation even more convenient than before.

Cheap power also made interurban electric trains economically feasible. Steam trains were used for long distance hauls, but for short runs with frequent stops, something else was needed. An electric road, with its fast starts and stops and cheap power, could make the frequent local stops profitable.

The "Grand Electrical Carnival" of September 9, 1895, literally electrified Sacramento. Citizens celebrated the successful transmission of power from Folsom Dam, 22 miles away. Arc lights decorated buildings, and a parade featuring lighted floats and streetcars was the focus of the carnival. Sixty thousand visitors responded to this invitation and joined the celebration. Courtesy, Herb Caplan Collection, SMHD

The novelty of cheap electricity led to excessive displays such as this one. On September 9, 1895, California's admission day, the "Grand Electrical Carnival" lit up John Breuner's furniture company building at 6th and K streets. Other prominent city buildings, including the capitol, were also illuminated. Courtesy, Sacramento City Library Collection, SMHD

Streetcars were a familiar sight to Sacramentans between the early 1890s and the late 1940s. These two pages show a few of the cars that have graced the city's streets.

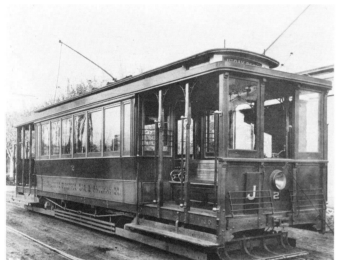

Top: Sacramento Northern Railroad Company (David Joslyn Collection); **above,** Sacramento Electric, Gas, and Railway Company (Ralph Shaw Collection); **above right,** Central Electric Railway Company (California State Library Collection); **right,** Sacramento Electric, Gas, and Railway Company (California State Library Collection)

Left: Central Electric Railway Company (California State Library Collection); **below left,** Pacific Gas and Electric Company car barns (Pacific Gas and Electric Company Collection); **below,** Pacific Gas and Electric Company (Brian Thompson Collection); **bottom,** Sacramento Streetcar Company (Brian Thompson Collection)

All pictures courtesy of the Sacramento Museum and History Division

The intersection of 8th and K streets was a busy place during the early years of the century. Left to right can be seen cars of the city's electric streetcar system, the California Traction Company, and the Sacramento Northern. The lines converged one block to the north at 8th and J streets where a switch enabled the cars of the traction company to change direction. Too many cars on the downtown streets finally caused serious traffic congestion problems. Courtesy, David Joslyn Collection, SMHD

The Southern Pacific Company monopolized railroad traffic out of Sacramento. This angered some local businessmen, and in an election on October 22, 1907, Sacramentans approved a proposal by the Western Pacific Railway Company to begin competition with Southern Pacific. The company's first freight train crossed town along 19th Street on November 13, 1909. In August of the next year the Western Pacific depot opened at 19th and J streets. Courtesy, Norman L. Wilson

In 1905 Henry Butters, who had built railroads in South Africa and Mexico, started building the Sacramento Northern, an electric railroad, from Chico to Sacramento. In spite of political controversy, competition with Western Pacific, and the 1907 floods, the railroad to Sacramento was completed on September 1, 1907, just in time for the State Fair. Trains left the depot on 8th Street to reach Chico in 2-1/2 hours.

Rail travel was further improved in 1907 when the M Street Bridge was opened, adding another crossing over the Sacramento River. Between 1910 and 1915 a burst of railroad building multiplied lines to Sacramento. The Sacramento Terminal Company completed a belt line around the outskirts of the city to serve industrial areas and canneries. The California Traction Company built a line from Sacramento to Stockton, while the Sacramento Northern extended its rails to the Bay Area.

While the Southern Pacific line carried most of the transcontinental traffic, Western Pacific gave the valley a second transcontinental line. At the height of the railroad era, Southern Pacific had up to 23 arrivals and departures daily. The total arrivals and departures in the city were up to 150 daily, or an average of eight per line. Rails made the whole valley tributary to Sacramento, aiding the agricultural industry—particularly fruit and milk commerce—while steam and electricity combined to make Sacramento the distribution center of Northern California.

Sacramento citizens ushered in the new century with exuberance, as people came from all around Northern California for the Street Fair and Floral Parade of 1900. The passenger station was decorated inside and out. In the evenings every street lamp along L and N streets was lighted, and hundreds of incandescent lights were draped on trees and buildings. The Capitol Mall was turned into a carnival midway, and merchants set up displays along L and N. On the first day of the celebration a large crowd gathered on the capitol grounds for the coronation of the May Queen.

The next day the Chinese community put on a spectacular show—the Chinese Dragon Parade. Hundreds of Chinese men and women dressed in their finest silks and brocades to accompany the 100-foot-long dragon.

The Capital City Wheelmen formed during the bicycling craze of the 1880s. They organized and entered sprint and long-distance races. The Capital City Wheelmen Racing Team, shown here, was the state champion for the 1903-1904 season. The Wheelmen also lobbied for road surface improvements. Courtesy, Sacramento City-County Library Collection, SMHD

Celebrants were treated to yet another parade that day. In the Floral Parade the members of two bicycle clubs—the Capital City and the Oak Park Wheelmen—led a procession of flower-bedecked bicycles, horses, carriages, floats, and marching bands. One of the bicycle club members drove a novel vehicle—an automobile.

That September the San Francisco agent for one of the new models, the Locomobile, brought his auto to the 1900 State Fair and gave a demonstration run around the mile-long track at Agricultural Park. First, the pacers and trotters ran the mile in 2 minutes, 15 seconds. Then it was the auto's turn. It went almost as fast as the horses, posting a time of 2 minutes, 23 seconds (nearly 30 miles an hour). Two years later a grand total of two automobiles took part in the May celebration.

The automobile changed the way people used their leisure time. This 1913 photograph shows the Taketa family enjoying an excursion in one of Sacramento's parks. The growing popularity of automobile touring paved the way for road improvements. Courtesy, Henry Taketa

Above: Before the introduction of gasoline-powered trucks, retail stores such as Weinstock, Lubin, and Company used horse-drawn wagons to deliver merchandise. Colonel Harris Weinstock received this view on a postcard during a visit to Australia in 1909. Courtesy, Ralph Shaw Collection, SMHD

Above right: By the 1920s horsepower had replaced horses. This photograph shows the delivery truck of Breuner's, one of Sacramento's oldest retail outlets. The delivery men are unloading a Wedgewood range in Sacramento. Courtesy, David Joslyn Collection, SMHD

Early in 1903 Joseph Schnerr, a planing factory employee, leased a shop at 10th and J for the sale of automobiles and bicycles. Apparently there was little profit from the automobiles. When Schnerr left the business two years later, his partner kept the bicycle line but dropped the automobiles. By 1904 there were still only 27 automobiles registered in Sacramento County.

On the weekend after Thanksgiving in 1904, race car driver Barney Oldfield sparked excitement with his 48-horsepower Green Dragon and traveling road show. Several racers had driven up from Stockton for the show, and after dining at one of the downtown restaurants on Saturday afternoon, the racers got into their cars and drove along 2nd Street, purposely backfiring to create a racket. Startled horses reared and whinnied and pedestrians scurried for cover. One of the Stockton racers darted up K Street in his red Pope Toledo at 40 miles per hour. When the driver finally stopped, a police officer arrested him for "scorching."

The following Sunday, December 4, hundreds of people gathered at Agricultural Park for the speed show. In a preliminary performance racer Charley Burman drove his 24-horsepower Blue Streak around the one-mile track at 60 miles per hour. The *Union* reporter who accompanied him gave the following account of his experience:

> *Although the first mile was traveled in comparatively slow time, I was sufficiently impressed with the necessity of clinging on. A cloud of dust, arising from a track that I considered wet, was a phenomenon that engrossed my attention until I had perfected my hold. After that the track seemed rushing forward to meet us, and the air struck me in the face with short, sharp puffs.*
>
> *At the first turn we headed straight for the outer fence, as it seemed, and, concluding that the driver had lost control, I resigned myself to the inevitable. As we neared the whitewashed rail there was a sudden veering of the wheels, the machine slid around until it was headed for the stretch, and my composure resumed sway.*
>
> *After that is was enjoyable. The gray track rushed past as if it were in motion; the punishment inflicted by the rushes of air diminished, and the jar and jolt became more and more imperceptible as the speed increased. Except for the feeling of danger that accompanied each turn in the track, the sensation was absolutely pleasant, and, although I would not care to travel again at a pace so reckless, I enjoyed every instant of the ride.*

But Sacramento's early preoccupation with the automobile was to be interrupted by events in San Francisco and the subsequent statewide political changes. At 5:15 a.m. on April 18, 1906, Sacramentans were roused from their beds by a violent minute-long shaking. Many ran out into the streets in their nightclothes. No one was injured and not so much as a pane of glass was broken, but a little later the city learned that its neighbors on the coast had sustained massive damages. Most of San Francisco had been destroyed by the earthquake and the subsequent fire. To the north, the little town of Santa Rosa was devastated. To the south, Stanford University, San Jose, and Santa Cruz all reported extensive damage and numerous deaths.

Hundreds of Sacramentans beseiged newspaper and telegraph offices for news about Bay Area friends and relatives. The next morning citizens massed at the courthouse, raised $50,000 within the hour, and organized a relief committee to send supplies to San Francisco. Sutter's Fort, which had sheltered immigrants in the years before the Gold Rush, was pressed into service as a relief camp for earthquake refugees. Sacramento hereby repaid its debt of 1852, when the people of San Francisco helped it rebuild after flood and fire, and with the help of Sacramento and other California cities, San Francisco started rebuilding within a week.

By destroying California's largest seaport city and commercial center, the earthquake shook up politics as well. During the rebuilding process a group of reformists calling themselves Lincoln-Roosevelt Republicans quickly gained a foothold. Vowing to wipe out corruption, they ran candidates for offices at city, county, and state levels. People in Sacramento took a special interest in this political revolt, for its leader, Hiram Johnson, had been a prominent citizen and attorney of the capital city before leaving to practice law in San Francisco. When he ran for governor in 1910, Johnson campaigned up and down California in a red Locomobile convertible. Using the slogan, "Kick the Southern Pacific Railroad out of politics," he won the governorship, and the reformists took control of the senate and assembly.

Under the leadership of Governor Johnson the 1911 legislature drew up a slate of reforms (23 propositions) to be ratified by the voters. Among them were the initiative and referendum, designed to give voters a direct voice in the lawmaking process, and the recall, by which voters could remove public officials—including judges—from office. These won by large majorities.

The hottest issue on that ballot proposed to upset traditional relationships between the sexes while doubling the number of eligible voters in the state. Proposition 4 on the ballot, Constitutional Amendment No. 8, asked the

Constructed in 1909, this City Hall faces the north side of City Plaza. This 1917 photograph, probably taken from the 926 J Street building, shows the surrounding residential area. The building, which continues to house the city council, is now in the middle of a largely commercial neighborhood. Courtesy, Norman Silsbee Collection, SMHD

all-male electorate to give women the vote.

It was appropriate that a governor from Sacramento should return to the capital and propose women's suffrage, for Sacramento women had campaigned for the right to vote for more than 40 years. Led by Mrs. L.G. Waterhouse, pioneer midwife and hydropathic physician, the Sacramento Woman's Suffrage Association held a convention in December 1871 at which national leader Susan B. Anthony spoke to an enthusiastic audience. In 1872 suffragists persuaded the state legislature to consider the issue. After lively debates and public hearings, the legislature concluded regretfully that women would not be likely to vote in the near future, for "tradition and prejudice would be hard to overcome."

Interest waxed and waned over the next 40 years. Suffrage organizations had kept the question alive by petitioning the legislature annually, but it was the general shake-up in politics that stirred the first real hope of getting the vote. As the day of the special election approached, suffragists held rallies, debates, and parades. Many civic leaders endorsed the cause. The Sacramento Equal Suffrage League held a large rally in the high school, and the *Bee* ran a series of editorial cartoons in favor. The *Union* urged voters to support the cause "as a simple matter of justice."

On the other side, a leading anti-suffragist, Col. John P. Irish, assailed the suffrage cause, claiming it was led by "uneasy political women, representing but two-tenths of the women of California." He urged his audience to "stand by your guns, stand by your homes, stand by the eight-tenths of the women of California, and vote no on the amendment."

On election day, October 10, 1911, Sacramento suffragists handed out cards and literature at each of the city's polls. One of the women drove her automobile from precinct to precinct, carrying literature and relief workers. The following morning the *Union* banner-headlined the election results:

SUFFRAGE IS IN DOUBT, OTHER AMENDMENTS WIN

The early returns looked grim for the suffragists, and that evening the *Bee* announced:

WOMAN SUFFRAGE IS DEFEATED IN CALIFORNIA BY 5000

But as ballot counting continued, the tide began to turn. On the second day after the election, returns from Los Angeles, Alameda and Shasta counties came in with majorities for suffrage. The *Union* bannered:

SUFFRAGE CAUSE NOW APPEARS VICTORIOUS

Mrs. Lillian C. Hough, president of the Sacramento Equal Suffrage League, declared, "I am too happy for words. We have worked against great odds, and we have met with much strong opposition. So now if we have won we will feel all the more appreciative of our victory."

The *Bee* that evening confirmed the news:

CALIFORNIA WOMEN WIN SUFFRAGE!

California thereby became the sixth state to grant woman suffrage. Nine years later, on August 26, 1920, the 19th Amendment extended the right to vote to women throughout the United States.

The automobile was symbolic of new freedom for women, for it enabled them to move about the city without depending on others to provide them with transportation. This was especially true after the self-starter eliminated the need for cranking.

By 1911 the automobile was on the road to replacing the horse, and Sacramento agencies sold Fords, Maxwells, Chalmers-Detroits, Thomas Flyers, and Oldsmobiles.

By 1914 there were 3,419 automobiles registered in Sacramento County—about one for every 20 citizens. The changeover from the horse to the automobile had a wide-ranging impact on Sacramento, for at the turn of the century the city was dotted with blacksmith shops, horseshoers, harness and saddlery makers, feed lots, and carriage and wagonmakers. Hundreds of workers belonged to trades associations such as carriage builders, team drivers, stage hands, blacksmiths, and horseshoers.

A dozen years later horseshoers had vanished from the city and the number of blacksmith shops had declined from 18 to 14. Feed lots were reduced from 23 in 1902 to 11 in 1912. Some business owners simply closed shop. Others diversified. Many bicycle and carriage shops added automobile sales, repairs, or accessories to their services. A.A. Van Voorhies, one of the oldest harness and saddle makers, switched from making leather saddles to selling leather shoes. Palm Iron and Carriage Works eased out of the carriage business and started making structural steel beams for bridges and high-rise buildings. By 1912 there were 16 automobile agencies, one automobile assembly plant, and 11 garages for storage and maintenance.

County roads gave Sacramento access to points north, east, and south, but motorists traveling west during the winter months encountered a major obstacle. After the first few rains the Yolo Basin overflowed, creating a vast inland sea, and the detour by way of Stockton took several hours.

Sacramentans had campaigned for good roads long before the automobile. When the bicycle became popular in the 1880s, a group of local enthusiasts formed the Capital City Wheelmen. During races and long-distance rides they became acutely aware of road conditions. In 1892 two

The seemingly ubiquitous car lot rode its product's coattails into the man-made geography of America. This Chevrolet agency, operated by Matthew and Robert Batey, proved that even a small town like Elk Grove could support an auto agency. The Batey Brothers' establishment was located on the town's eastern edge. Courtesy, Sacramento City-County Library Collection, SMHD

Winter flooding annually cut off access to Sacramento from the west. A bond approved by voters in 1910 funded the construction of the Yolo Causeway. The causeway, seen here under construction in 1915, raised State Highway 40 to guarantee year-round traffic flow. Courtesy, California State Archives Collection, SMHD

members of the Wheelmen toured the San Joaquin and Yolo areas to document the need for better roads. Forming a coalition with merchants, freighters, and farmers, the cyclists organized a Good Roads Convention in Sacramento in 1893.

Finance was the main obstacle to road improvement. The first time city and county voters approved a bond issue, the state supreme court ruled that the county had no legal right to bond itself and the city for a county road. The voters tried again in 1907. An overwhelming majority favored the roads, 2,550 voting for the issue and only 317 against. This time their vote prevailed, and the county applied macadam surfacing to the main roads. And in 1911 two new bridges were built over the American River (one at 12th Street and one at H Street), connecting Sacramento to points north and east.

The state created the California Highway Commission in 1909 and submitted a bond issue to voters the following year. The major project financed by this bond issue was the Yolo Causeway, an elevated two-lane roadway supported by a wooden trestle. When the Yolo Causeway was opened in 1916, Sacramentans gained year-round access to the Bay Area.

Sacramento hosted a grand three-day celebration beginning May 12, 1916, to mark the completion of the new causeway. Motorists decorated their automobiles for a jubilant parade through downtown Sacramento, and a crowd of dignitaries and citizens from both Sacramento and Yolo counties gathered on the capitol grounds to witness an event symbolizing the union of the two counties: the marriage of a Sacramento County woman and a Yolo County man.

Later that year Sacramento citizens passed another bond issue to improve roads and build bridges, and shortly thereafter the state incorporated the major county roads into the state system, leaving the county responsible only for the laterals.

The coming of war in 1917 affected the lives of many Sacramentans. Three years earlier Great Britain, France, and Russia had gone to war against Germany and Austria. When the United States joined the conflict on April 6, 1917, the Sacramento Chamber of Commerce held a patriotic mass meeting at the flag-bedecked Empress Theater (now the Crest) to recruit for the armed forces. Sacramento citizens quickly mobilized to support U.S. troops. They rolled bandages for the Red Cross, planted home gardens, and raised over $30 million in four Liberty Bond drives and the final Victory Drive. About 4,000 young men from Sacramento County served the colors; 100 never returned.

A year and a half later, early in the morning of Monday, November 11, 1918, the whistle of the city waterworks went off, followed by church bells, horns, and shouting. Newsboys hit the streets shouting, "Extra! Extra!" selling papers whose headlines screamed:

WAR ENDS

A *Union* reporter described the day-long jubilation:

> *Frenzied pandemonium loosed upon the wings of the sirens that shrieked forth through the blackness of midnight the sublime cry of liberty freed from the chains of the Hun, continued all day and far into the wee small hours of the morning. . .*
>
> *The deafening whirr of the whistles, the constant ringing of bells, the shrieking shrill of the automobile horns and the countless newsboys loudly peddling the extras in the streets, gave the sensational news to the capital city. The greatest of all wars had come to an end.*

When California's sons came marching home a few months later, the city prepared a gala reception. In April 1919, on the day after Easter, schoolchildren collected thousands of poppies from nearby fields and 100 young women in white dresses scattered them, making a golden carpet along the street between the railway station and the capitol building. Bands played and flags waved as the soldiers marched from the station to the capitol, where they were feted with music and speeches before journeying to the Presidio at San Francisco for another rousing welcome.

After the war the pace of life quickened as automobiles and trucks finally replaced horses on city streets. In 1920 there was only about one automobile for every six people, but by the end of the decade the ratio was about one to three. And traffic moved faster. In earlier years a rider or teamster going more than five miles an hour in town risked a ticket for "furious driving," but when gasoline-powered buggies took over, 20 to 25 miles per hour became the norm.

During the postwar years Sacramento citizens voted bonds to build a new high school and revive the fledgling junior college, which had closed briefly near the end of the war when all of its male students had gone into the armed services. The junior college (now Sacramento City College), a pioneer among institutions of higher learning in California, was organized in 1916 by Sacramento High School teacher Belle Cooledge; it remained the only public postsecondary institution in the county for the next 30 years. Cooledge was appointed dean of the junior college in 1920 when it reopened in its new location; a wing of the new high school at 34th and Y. Six years later the college moved to its own campus on Freeport Boulevard.

The city's geography changed rapidly as large office buildings rose upwards along J, K, and L streets. In 1927 the city built a magnificent theater to honor its war dead. Memorial Auditorium attracted a wide range of events, including lectures, concerts, dances, pageants, conventions, boxing matches, operas, and graduation exercises.

While the automobile opened new vistas in everyday living, another development, moving pictures, enlarged the world of fantasy. In the early 1900s many theaters showed short features on a screen, accompanied by live organ or piano music. By 1913 ten theaters lined K Street, with several others a short distance away. Many started out with live shows and plays, but later added movies. In the 1920s most of the theaters showed silent films, and streetcar lines and cheap admission attracted the young set to Saturday matinees.

Above left: Built in 1913 at 1013 K Street, the Empress Theater was one of Sacramento's best-known vaudeville houses. The rise in the popularity of movies caused this theater to be replaced by the Hippodrome. In 1947 the Hippodrome Theater was renamed the Crest. Courtesy, California State Library Collection, SMHD

Above: During World War I, women in Sacramento volunteered for non-traditional work to support the war effort. These women, shown standing in front of a pile of scrap metal, worked at the Southern Pacific yards. The involvement of women in the work force was not as extensive as it was during the Second World War. This photo was taken on August 30, 1917. Courtesy, David Joslyn Collection, SMHD

Following World War I, Sacramento's economy experienced a burst of growth. This view, looking west from 12th and J streets, shows two of the city's skyscrapers—the California Life Insurance building at 926 J Street, and the Elks building at the corner of 11th and J. Courtesy, David Joslyn Collection, SMHD

As the myths and magic of Hollywood flourished, major studios built grand theaters in which to showcase their productions. The Fox Senator and the Hippodrome were among the finest in Sacramento. But the grandest of all was the Alhambra. Conceived by banker and businessman George Peltier, the palatial playhouse was modeled after the world-famous castle in Granada, Spain, with Moorish architecture, gardens, courtyards, and fountains. On opening night—Saturday, September 24, 1927—the city turned out in its finest array. Hollywood celebrities joined a host of dignitaries and civic leaders for the glittering celebration. The *Bee* exclaimed, "Nowhere else in all the world is there anything quite like this new playhouse."

By 1929 there seemed to be no limits to continued prosperity. Sacramento merchants advertised in the papers:

We Believe in Sacramento!

Who dares to doubt that the future of Sacramento promises continued growth and augmented prosperity? Basing our faith on our city's many material advantages and the progressive spirit which animates its citizens, we look forward to still greater achievements in every form of social and industrial activity.

An item on the financial page on October 29, 1929, cast a disturbing shadow, but it was quickly dismissed as a temporary aberration. The New York and San Francisco stock markets skidded downward as panicky traders sought to unload their stocks at rock-bottom prices. After an apparent recovery the next day, a Yale economist predicted that the bear market had reached bottom, and the *Union* reassured its readers of the basic stability of the economy in an editorial which bore the headline:

NO WAY NOW BUT UP

During the 1920s K Street dominated the business district. Theaters, restaurants, shops, and hotels flourished. This view, looking west toward the intersection of 10th and K streets, shows the Hotel Sacramento and Hotel Land on the left. The Hippodrome Theater on the right at 1013 K Street still exists today as the Crest Theater. Courtesy, David Joslyn Collection, SMHD

Perhaps the grandest of all of Sacramento's movie palaces was the Alhambra Theater which was modeled after the Moorish masterpiece in Granada, Spain. The theater opened on September 24, 1927. Thirty-first Street was renamed Alhambra Boulevard in its honor. This photograph shows the theater at the lavish 1936 world premiere of "Sutter's Gold." Courtesy, California Department of Parks and Recreation Collection, SMHD

Chapter 6
NEW VISTAS
1930-1970

During the Depression the federal government poured millions of dollars into Sacramento's economy, creating and sustaining growth. World War II brought two air bases and an army depot into the area, along with thousands of military personnel. The postwar period saw the population of the unincorporated county surpass that of the city, and a corresponding growth in residential and commercial developments followed.

Sacramento, buffered by the diversity of its economic base, felt the effects of the Great Depression gradually. But as the Depression deepened, farmers found it harder to sell their crops, canneries hired fewer workers, and merchants sold less merchandise.

Between 1930 and 1932, automobile sales in Sacramento dropped from 5,560 per year to 2,236. At the same time a local welfare unit which had fed 354 families a month quadrupled its caseload to 1,503 families. The Salvation Army, which had prepared an average of 220 meals a day in 1931, gave out nearly triple that amount—625 meals a day—in 1932. With no federal funds available, local relief agencies were hard pressed to aid newcomers drifting into the valley seeking jobs.

Beginning in October 1931, a half dozen shantytowns, known as "Hoovervilles," grew up along the Sacramento and American rivers. The largest had more than 500 shanties put together from cardboard, tin, boxes, and scraps salvaged from the nearby city dump. Only three had indoor plumbing. In the summer of 1935 the city closed down the Hoovervilles and local agencies helped the residents find other living quarters.

Early in 1933 two Sacramento banks failed, depriving 4,000 depositors of their savings and checking accounts. On January 21 the California National Bank and its affiliate, the California Trust & Savings, planned to open for business as usual. A large crowd of depositors, alarmed by rumors, had gathered to withdraw their funds, and an hour later both banks closed up and posted suspension notices on their doors. Amidst a storm of accusations and recriminations, a grand jury later found the bank directors innocent of criminal action but guilty of mismanagement.

The Great Depression focused attention on the nation's economic system. In the summer of 1934, a general strike said to have been led by socialists and communists paralyzed San Francisco. Fear of a similar strike gripped Sacramento. As the Bay Area strike ended, Sacramento police raided Communist headquarters and six of the shacks in the largest of the Hoovervilles, arresting 24 Communist party members on charges of criminal syndicalism (advocating violence to overthrow industry and government).

On several previous occasions the city had felt the disruptive results of radical rhetoric. In the summer of 1894, at the height of the fruit season, two thousand Southern Pacific shop workers went on strike. Strangely, they had no grievance against the local shop. Working conditions were good and wages high. The American Railway Union, led by socialist Eugene V. Debs, had ordered all of its members to refuse to work on any train pulling a Pullman car, because it wanted to bring the Pullman Company in Chicago to terms. The Pullman Strike crippled the entire Southern Pacific System.

Two weeks after the strike began, federal troops arrived in Sacramento to get the U.S. mails, which had stopped because of the strikes, moving again. On the morning of July 11, Overland No. 4 rolled out of the depot under federal guard. At the Yolo bypass, a group of strikers derailed the train, killing engineer Sam Clark and four soldiers.

The strike paralyzed the Sacramento Valley for three weeks, and when it was over, a quarter of the city's households had lost three weeks' pay. Merchants and manufacturers had lost business. Seasonal workers counting on summer employment had been turned away. Farmers had lost the better part of their first good fruit crop in two years. Federal troops had occupied the city for more than a week—"a situation," the *Sacramento Union* commented, "that is humiliating to local pride."

Citizens were outraged at the calamity visited upon them. A group of

Facing page: Charles Lindbergh visited Sacramento in September 1927. A group of local military pilots escorted the "Lone Eagle" to the ground. Lindbergh's visit stimulated interest in aviation and aided the drive for a municipal airport. Courtesy, California State Library Collection, SMHD

During the 1930s one of Sacramento's major industries was canning fruits and vegetables from the Central Valley. During the Depression the canneries provided jobs, although only for the summer season. This 1931 photograph shows the Del Monte Cannery during the peach harvest. Courtesy, Mike Geary Collection, SMHD

civic leaders denounced "the principle that any organization should be permitted to paralyze the business of the country to force some particular individual to terms."

Some 20 years later, in the spring of 1914, Sacramento played unwilling host to an army of political protesters marching somewhat loosely under the banner of the Industrial Workers of the World, commonly known as the I.W.W. or the "Wobblies." A self-appointed labor leader, General Charles T. Kelley, had gathered about 1,500 unemployed men from the coastal and valley towns, intending to march on Washington and lead a workers' rebellion. After minor skirmishes with authorities in San Francisco and Oakland, "Kelley's Army" arrived in Sacramento on Friday, March 6. The city put them up over the weekend on a fenced lot near the railroad depot. On Monday morning the *Sacramento Union* reported:

> *The situation on the sandlot is a mixture of the ludicrous and the threatening. Despite the effort of the army to levy on the city for some $15,000, Sacramento turned out yesterday to view the encampment as if it had been a county fair.*

Rather than give in to the army's demands for food and train fare to continue east, the city arrested Kelley, and used a force of police, deputies, and firemen to drive the leaderless mob back over the river to Yolo County, where the men eventually dispersed.

When the nation was eight months into World War I, Sacramentans were awakened near midnight on December 17, 1917, by an explosion. The morning paper reported that unknown terrorists, "almost certainly agents of the German government with I.W.W. affiliations," had dynamited the governor's mansion. No one was injured, but citizens were alarmed by the assassination attempt. A week later police arrested two I.W.W. leaders driving a delivery wagon with nine sticks of dynamite hidden in a box of soap. After police rounded up 28 more I.W.W. members, newspapers credited sharp detective work for foiling a plot to dynamite and burn the city.

When the specter of Communism re-emerged during the Depression, Republicans made political hay, branding Democratic policies Communist-inspired. Wildcat strikes by farm workers and the general strike in San Francisco had convinced many that the threat was real. Newspaper headlines during the gubernatorial campaign of 1934 reflected the general alarm:

Troops from Mather Field lined up at the rear of the old post office at 7th and K streets to escort the payroll to the Army Air Corps training base in 1918. The transportation of such large sums of cash always required protection. Courtesy, Eleanor McClatchy Collection, SMHD

RED PLAN FOR DRIVE IN CAPITAL
REPORT SAYS 2000 SYMPATHIZERS OF RADICALS
WILL GATHER HERE
POLICE PREPARE FOR COMMUNIST MARCH ON CITY

After incumbent governor Frank Merriam, a conservative Republican, easily defeated Democratic challenger Upton Sinclair, a leading socialist, the "Red Scare" died away.

In Sacramento—and most of the nation—the economic situation had begun to improve the year before, when Democrat Franklin D. Roosevelt took office as President. Roosevelt had campaigned in Sacramento on September 22, 1932, promising an enthusiastic crowd "not a mere change of party, but a change of principles: a new deal."

From 1933 to 1939, New Deal agencies poured a million dollars a year into Sacramento, putting thousands of people to work. The Public Works Administration (PWA) and its successor, the Works Progress Administration (WPA) gave loans and grants to public agencies. Among the beneficiaries of these federal funding projects were 46 new public buildings, the new city high school, the junior college, a city-wide water project, county school districts, the municipal airport, the fairgrounds, parks, bridges, and hundreds of miles of roads.

On December 15, 1935, the Tower Bridge across the Sacramento River at M Street was opened to the public. This concrete and metal structure has become a symbol of Sacramento. The Capitol on the east and the Tower Bridge on the west define Capitol Mall. This photograph shows the procession that marked the bridge's opening. Courtesy, Cal Trans Collection, SMHD

While the nation was struggling to free itself from the Depression the international situation deteriorated rapidly and war broke out in Europe in 1939. However, people were stunned when the news came over the radio on December 7, 1941, that Japanese planes were bombing Pearl Harbor. The broad Pacific Ocean no longer protected Americans from enemy attack. For the next three nights Sacramento residents experienced blackouts—lights in the city were turned off so that an enemy pilot could not identify a target. Even the dome of the Capitol was darkened. The city was organized into 20 air raid districts and eventually enlisted 800 air raid wardens (civilians trained to enforce blackouts, put out incendiary fires, and handle emergencies during alerts and raids).

Immediately after the attack on Pearl Harbor, a number of Japanese Americans placed full-page ads in newspapers declaring their loyalty to the United States. President Roosevelt and Governor Culbert Olson urged citizens not to judge all Japanese by the actions of the Japanese government, but the voices of reason were soon muffled. The American Legion and hundreds of thousands of terrified people demanded the removal of all possible enemy spies—Germans, Italians, and Japanese—from the vulnerable western regions of the United States and Canada.

Under the Presidents' authorization, the Western Defense Command in March 1942 ordered the evacuation of Japanese residents, justifying the removal of citizens from their homes "for their own protection," because "Occidentals cannot tell a loyal Japanese from a disloyal one," and because "the very fact that no sabotage has taken place to date is a disturbing and confirming indication that such action will be taken." In the prevailing climate of near-hysteria, these fallacious assertions were widely accepted as truthful and convincing.

Many Japanese families had settled in the city and in the Florin, Freeport, and Pocket districts south of town. (Sacramento County had the third largest Japanese population on the West Coast.) On May 11, 1942, Sacramento's Japanese residents gathered in Memorial Auditorium to be registered. The roll numbered 1,014 families, representing 3,800 men, women, and children. Two days later they were sent to a hastily-constructed assembly center on a 150-

Freeport is a quiet community on the Sacramento River a few miles south of Sacramento. The town is beginning to feel the pressures of Sacramento's southward expansion. This photograph shows the less hectic atmosphere at the turn of the century. Courtesy, California State Library Collection, SMHD

acre site at Walerga, the little railroad stop a few miles northeast of the city.

After a while the Japanese were sent to more permanent camps farther inland, where they stayed for a year or two until national paranoia died down. Many returned to the Sacramento Valley after the war. Meanwhile, Camp Walerga became Camp Kohler, and served as a transition center for an altogether different section of the populace dislocated because of the war—military draftees.

The war became a part of daily life on the Home Front: each day's newspapers carried stories of battles, shoppers counted out their ration stamps, schoolchildren collected scrap metal, and uniformed soldiers and sailors became a familiar sight on downtown streets. The war also affected a special group of business houses which had been a traditional part of city life since the days of the Gold Rush: brothels. Public Law 163, signed by President Roosevelt on July 11, 1941, outlawed prostitution near military bases. The ban was generally ignored until May 1943, when the threat of having the whole city declared off limits to military personnel precipitated their closing.

In May 1945 Germany surrendered, but Japan held out. After President Harry Truman announced the Japanese surrender on August 14, the *Bee* described the city's jubilant response:

> Minutes after the peace announcement, hilariously happy throngs took over K Street and in a short time servicemen who "directed" traffic had all movement snarled. The police blocked off the center section and the pedestrians took over the downtown section, staging the most boisterous celebration Sacramento has witnessed.

The most lasting legacy of World War II for the Sacramento Valley was the enormous and permanent expansion of the suburban area. Two air bases, activated when the war broke out in Europe, formed the nucleii for development to the north and east. After the war the attention of builders and developers shifted from the relatively small area enclosed by the city limits to the vast reaches in the northeast section of the county.

The northeast suburbs are concentrated in a pie-shaped wedge of territory of approximately 100 square miles, with the city at the far western tip. The area is roughly bounded by Highway 80 (which leads to Reno) on the north and Highway 50 (which leads to South Lake Tahoe) on the south. Highway 50 also roughly—very roughly—parallels the American River as far as Folsom.

The first of the two air bases to be activated was Mather Air Field, located due east of the city and just south of Highway 50. It had been built as an aviation school for World War I flyers in 1918, but had been closed shortly afterwards. It was re-opened in 1936. Within a few years it hosted thousands of military personnel and employed many civilian workers.

The other air base, McClellan Field, was established in 1937 and opened two years later, diagonally northeast of the city and just north of Highway 80. By 1943 it had grown to more than 18,000 military and civilian employees. The neighboring communities of Del Paso Heights and North Highlands both grew accordingly. The then-separately incorporated town of North Sacramento also felt the impact, as thousands of newcomers created a demand for housing and stimulated business in the private sector.

A third military installation, the Sacramento Signal Depot, was established in 1941 for the storage and repair of army equipment, especially communications equipment. Although its impact was not as dramatic as that of

When the Army opened an aviation training school in Sacramento in June 1918, many of the instructors came from Ellington Field in Texas. Carl Mather, second lieutenant and pioneer aviator, had been killed at Ellington in January 1918. The new field was named after the young pilot. Mather was closed from 1923 until 1935 when the Wilcox national air defense bill provided funds to renovate the base. Mather formally reopened in 1936. Courtesy, Silver Wings Collection, SMHD

Mather and McClellan, it too added to the population and economic base.

After a brief flirtation with de-militarization at the end of the war, the United States quickly became caught up in the Cold War with Russia. Instead of closing down as at the end of the First World War, the military bases remained at full strength. They were soon joined in the valley by private industries with government contracts. Shortly after the Korean conflict broke out in 1950, several aerospace corporations, including Aerojet and McDonnell-Douglas, expanded their facilities to the Sacramento Valley. The barren land covered with dredger tailings just to the east of Mather Air Base became a testing site for rocket engines and flight systems.

In 1957 the Russians launched Sputnik, the world's first artificial satellite, and the space race was on. The United States started pouring huge sums of money into defense and aerospace industries. Much of that federal money landed in the Sacramento Valley. Before this time there had been only a few settlements in the northeast area, and they were separated from each other by miles of two-lane roads meandering through orchards and farmland.

The town of Folsom, terminus of the first railroad built in the valley, had been established in 1855. This area began as a Mexican land grant, the 35,000 acre *Rancho de los Americanos,* several years before the Gold Rush. William A. Leidesdorf, a mulatto from the Danish West Indies, owned the land from 1844 until his death in 1848. A few years later, Captain Joseph L. Folsom, who came to California during the Mexican War, bought the property from Leidesdorf's heirs. Folsom and railroad builder Theodore Judah founded the town of Folsom near the American River at the northeastern tip of the land grant late in 1855. Upon completion of the Sacramento Valley Railroad, the town became a lively stagecoach and freighting center.

In the 1880s and 1890s a number of fruit colonies were established in the area west of Folsom, roughly within the upper reaches of the pie-shaped wedge between present-day Highways 80 and 50: Fair Oaks, Citrus Heights,

In 1951 the Aerojet General Corporation moved into rural Sacramento County, east of the city, and established a rocket research facility there. During the 1950s and 1960s the company was one of the county's major employers, and Aerojet's presence contributed to the suburbanization of the eastern part of the county. Courtesy, Aerojet Collection, SMHD

and Orangevale. The town of Carmichael was started in 1909 by D.W. Carmichael, a Sacramento real estate developer. By 1960 Fair Oaks, Citrus Heights, and Carmichael had grown to about 20,000 residents each. Orangevale, a little more distant from the air bases and the city, had about 11,000. The community of Rancho Cordova, off Highway 50 just north of Mather, was subdivided in 1953; it had grown to 13,000 by 1960.

Watching the remarkable population growth, the city began eyeing the area for annexation, and numerous annexation proposals were put before voters during this time period. Most of them were turned down.

The city had made its first annexation of surrounding territory back in 1911, increasing its population from 44,000 to over 60,000 and more than tripling its original four square miles of land area. Called the Oak Park annexation, the new acquisition consisted of an extensive arc of land generally east and south of the original city limits. Beginning at the Southern Pacific tracks along the American River to the north, it swept down through the residential areas and farmlands south to Sutterville Road.

In 1923 the levee along Y Street was leveled, and access to the south area became easier. About this time the city bought a large park site in the south area, using a bequest from William Land, who had owned two large and prosperous downtown hotels. Development of the beautiful park and golf course stimulated an extensive residential building program between Broadway (formerly Y Street) and Sutterville Road. The area around William Land Park soon became a fashionable neighborhood.

Development north of the American River had been blocked for many years by the single-family ownership of a Mexican land grant, the 44,000-acre *Rancho del Paso*, stretching from the bank of the river north to Rio Linda and east to Carmichael. Owner James Ben Ali Haggin had raised prize-winning thoroughbred horses on the land from the 1880s until after the turn of the century. The *Rancho* was sold in 1910 to a group of investors known as the Sacramento Valley Colonization Company, which in turn sold a portion to the city for recreational purposes (now Del Paso Park and the Haggin Oaks Golf Course). The greater part they divided between two purchasers, Charles Swanston & Son, owners of a cattle ranch in the south area (now William Land Park), and D.W. Johnston, a Bay Area real estate developer.

Prior to the establishment of the Sacramento Municipal Airport on Freeport Boulevard in 1930, the city was serviced by smaller air fields. In 1927 a section of Del Paso Park was improved to serve as a landing field. This view may be that air strip. Courtesy, David Joslyn Collection, SMHD

Johnston's son Carl started the town of North Sacramento, advertising country living "in the shade of the oaks—a ten-minute ride by rail to downtown Sacramento." When incorporated in 1925, North Sacramento had its own city hall, police office, fire department, library, and schools. It remained an independent entity until 1964, when, after heated controversy, its residents voted by a narrow margin to be annexed to the city—and that was Sacramento's last annexation.

The influx of population during the postwar years was similar to that which had occurred during the Gold Rush a hundred years before. The massive immigration created similar problems: provision of housing, food, goods, and services. This time, instead of individuals putting up tents, builders put up tracts. Subdivisions sprouted almost overnight. As in the Gold Rush days, merchants hastened to provide the food, goods, and services that were in demand. But instead of auctioning off their wares on the embarcadero, they displayed them in supermarkets and department stores.

Transportation, still a necessity, had changed its form. Newcomers, instead of stopping at the horse market to buy a four-footed conveyance to the mines, went to a new car showroom or a used car lot to purchase the

The automobile broadened the eating habits of Sacramentans. Drive-in restaurants, often with car-hop service, became popular. Andy's Drive-in at 2995 Freeport Boulevard appears to be surrounded by business in this 1941 photograph. Courtesy, Sacramento City-County Library Collection, SMHD

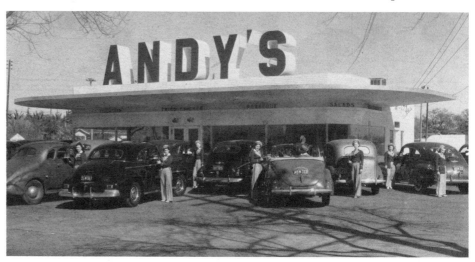

means to get to their new jobs. While the old city had been built to accommodate the horse and buggy, the new suburbs were designed for one- and two-car families. New homes had a garage attached to the house, and new shopping centers provided acres of free, off-street parking.

In 1945 the first suburban shopping center in California was opened at a location just beyond the northeastern limits of the city, a five-minute drive from McClellan Air Field. Other regional shopping centers followed, each larger and with different enticements than the one before. Air conditioned malls came into vogue beginning in 1968. The suburban shopping center reached the apex of development in the valley in 1972, with the grand opening of a gigantic, 86-acre mall in the far northeast area, just a ten-minute drive from either Mather or McClellan. When it opened, this shopping center featured four major department stores, plus 100 specialty shops in an air-conditioned, landscaped mall. Outside, a vast expanse of concrete offered parking for 6,500 automobiles.

During the postwar boom, as the burgeoning population took to the road to get to jobs and shopping centers, the two-lane country roads became woefully inadequate. Many were widened to four lanes in the 1950s. Freeways were built in the 1950s and 1960s as part of a nationwide freeway plan. By 1963 freeways led to Sacramento from all four directions of the compass. A commuter could get to the city limits from either the Citrus Heights area (Highway 80) or Folsom (Highway 50) in less than half an hour. The trip to San Francisco, which had taken eight or ten hours by riverboat in the Gold Rush period, now took a little more than an hour and a half.

In 1966 two federally-funded projects brought Sacramento closer to world markets: the deep-water Port of Sacramento and the Metropolitan Airport. Located west of the Sacramento River in Yolo County, the Port of Sacramento brings ocean-going ships inland to load bulk cargoes such as rice, wood chips, and a wide variety of exports. The same year that ships started using the new port, planes started flying out of the new Metropolitan Airport, about a 10-minute drive northwest of the city via Highway 5. This airport replaced the municipal airport on Freeport Boulevard, which is still used for smaller craft and private planes.

During the 1920s many Sacramentans, with the support of the Chamber of Commerce, pushed for better civilian aviation facilities to serve the city. In 1925 regular air mail service to Sacramento began along with air service between the city and San Francisco. The city selected a site south of town on Freeport Boulevard for a municipal airport. Dedicated in April 1930, the airfield exists today as the Executive Airport serving smaller aircraft. Courtesy, California State Library Collection, SMHD

Flooding remained a problem outside of the immediate city until the construction of Folsom Dam in the 1950s. This view was taken on January 22, 1943, looking east from the H Street Bridge toward the Horst Ranch hop fields. Today Campus Commons is located near this site. Courtesy, California State Library Collection, SMHD

A major change during the period of postwar growth was the shift in population power from the city to the suburbs. Although the county encompasses about 1,200 square miles (roughly the size of Rhode Island), for most of its history the greater part of the population had been concentrated in the few square miles bounded by the city limits. In 1940 the city population was 105,000; the rest of the county had only 65,000. During the 1950s the growth of the unincorporated area outpaced the city, matching and then surpassing it. By 1960 three-fifths of the population lived outside the city limits. By 1980 the city had 275,000 and the unincorporated area had over 500,000 in population. The greatest percentage of this new growth was in the pie-shaped northeast suburban section.

Additional population required additional municipal services, which were provided by combinations of government agencies and special assessment districts. The problem of the periodic flooding of the American River was finally brought under control in 1955, when Folsom Dam was built. A new sewage treatment plant was built in the mid-1950s (and another one in the 1980s). A new water treatment system was added in the 1960s.

The growth in the northeast suburbs was reflected by the growth of the San Juan Unified School District, a consolidation of many small districts covering about 75 percent of the 100-square-mile area between Highways 80 and 50. In just 15 years the number of schoolchildren grew from 8,000 in 1950 to 52,000 in 1965.

Space age industry required scientists, engineers, and skilled technicians, and Sacramento County responded by expanding its facilities for higher education. Sacramento Senator Earl Desmond in 1947 steered a bill through the legislature which created Sacramento State College (now California State University, Sacramento). By the 1980s it was serving some 22,000 students per year.

Among public two-year institutions, Sacramento City College had served the community alone for nearly 40 years, until American River Community College was built in 1956 in the north area near Highway 80. In 1970 Cosumnes River College opened to serve the south area, and by 1982 the three community colleges together had more than 40,000 students taking day and evening classes.

The process of suburbanization was accompanied by a renewed interest in parks and open spaces. The first parks had been created at the time the city was founded in 1849, when John Sutter, Jr. had designated a number of blocks for public use. Through the years many civic-minded citizens had donated land, labor, and materials to improve existing parks or add new ones.

After the automobile made pleasure trips practical for urban families, the city in 1919 bought a 40-acre parcel of land in the El Dorado National Forest, 85 miles to the east on Highway 50. With cabins, a dining-and-recreation hall, and mountain atmosphere, Camp Sacramento became a popular site for summer vacations.

Whereas Camp Sacramento took city dwellers to the country, the much more recently developed American River Parkway kept a strip of scenic country in the city and suburbs. The Parkway features a 23-mile bicycle trail following the picturesque course of the American River from its mouth at the Sacramento easterly to the Nimbus Dam fish hatchery near Folsom Lake. It was built between 1965 and 1975, following intensive lobbying by citizens and the securing of state and federal funds. As part of the parkway system, Discovery Park at the mouth of the American and C.M. Goethe and Ancil Hoffman parks in Carmichael offer facilities for picnicking, nature studies, and a variety of other recreational activities.

Parks, schools, shopping centers, highways, and subdivisions proliferated during the postwar years. But while the suburbs were blossoming, the central city was going to seed.

The popularity of automobile travel changed the hostelry habits of Americans. Travelers were attracted to the motels that were located along the major thoroughfares. The Florida Inn Motel, offering the economical convenience of kitchens, was located on Auburn Boulevard during the 1930s. Courtesy, Sacramento City-County Library Collection, SMHD

Chapter 7

COMMITMENT TO RENEWAL

1950-Present

Alarmed by the decay of the inner city, Sacramentans mobilized, first to clean up and build anew, and then to rescue their city's heritage. The State Capitol became a showpiece of historic preservation when it was restored to its turn-of-the-century magnificence, and Sacramento's downtown area became a model of urban restoration.

Ironically, the increase in people and automobiles which brought prosperity to the suburbs contributed to the decline of the downtown area. Traffic congestion practically strangled the central city, so customers fled to suburban shopping malls. Merchants followed the growing clientele to the suburbs. Downtown hotels suffered from the competition of suburban motels, and the big downtown movie theaters were replaced by drive-ins, mini-theaters in the shopping centers, and television sets in thousands of homes. By 1960, the future for downtown Sacramento looked bleak.

The riverfront area had started to decline in the 1920s. With the advent of the automobile and the corresponding reduction of rail and river transportation, stores and offices moved away from Front Street and eastward toward the Capitol. Old warehouses and cheap lodging places remained in the west end, attracting drifters, panhandlers, and alcoholics. As growth in the suburbs lured residents and shoppers away from the central city, and merchants moved out to follow them, vacant storefronts lined J and K streets.

No single property owner could stop the downward spiral. Although federal funds for urban renewal had been available since the Depression, it took concerted action by citizens and officials to secure and administer them. In 1950 the city council established the Sacramento Redevelopment Agency, which immediately launched a series of plans and studies to revitalize the city.

Four years later, a group of merchants and citizens banded together to form the Citizens Redevelopment Committee. They produced a local TV drama, "X Marks the Future," asking city voters to approve a $1.5 million bond issue for seed money for slum clearance in the west end, showing the potential for jobs, public health, and civic beautification. Opponents appealed to taxpayers' pocketbooks, claiming, "Approval of the bond issue will make it possible to acquire the property of many small businessmen, clear the land, and sell it. Private investors will purchase the property and redevelop it for personal gain."

Voters went to the polls on November 2, 1954. Voters in the west end, the area to be redeveloped, opposed it by a three-to-two margin and it went down to defeat. The *Bee* gave a brief assessment of the defeat's impact:

> *It kills, for the time being at least, plans for beautification and modernization of the entire west end of the city, shown by disease and crime statistics to be one of the worst slum areas in the nation.*

Five years later citizens regrouped under the banner of the Forward Sacramento Committee. Community leaders, city and county officials, business executives, and representatives from practically every segment of the community met at Memorial Auditorium for an unprecedented event, Decision Day Dinner, where they shared information, ideas, and planning concerns. Out of that April 1959 meeting came a renewed sense of dedication and a commitment to sound community planning.

Spurred by citizen interest and a combination of federal, state, and local funds, the Sacramento Redevelopment Agency by 1961 had cleared 15 blocks of dilapidated buildings, put in new utilities, and completed the first of the new buildings in its 62-block project area extending from the waterfront to 7th Street.

Throughout the Johnson administration, the Redevelopment Agency was able to secure substantial assistance from the Department of Housing and Urban Development. Thanks to the stimulus provided by federal funding, a

Facing page: By the 1920s Sacramento's west end had become skid row. The area was characterized by agricultural labor employment offices, warehouses, dilapidated hotels, and restaurants. The area posed a dilemma—the west end was the oldest area (except for Sutter's Fort) and one of the most architecturally interesting, but it was also the most run down. Courtesy, California State Library Collection, SMHD

The Sacramento Housing and Redevelopment Agency has helped to preserve the town of Locke as a living community. Locke was founded early in the 20th century as a Chinese agricultural community. The agency has raised funds for health and safety improvements and has coordinated more positive area zoning changes. Courtesy, City of Sacramento Collection, SMHD

number of apartment and condominium complexes arose. One of the most spectacular successes of this era was the Chinese Cultural Center, completed in 1973. It was located at I Street, where the Chinese had once lived in wooden houses until diffusing around the city at the turn of the century. The architecturally-unified complex reflects a tasteful blend of clean, modern lines with distinctively oriental embellishments. A flight of steps behind an elaborate wrought iron gate leads up to the Confucius Temple, built in 1959. Ramps and stairs lead down into a central courtyard at the original level of the city, eight feet below the present street level. High rise apartments are specially designed for the elderly, while shops and restaurants cater to the general public.

While the Chinese Cultural Center was taking shape on I Street, the commercial center two blocks away was also undergoing a transformation. The stretch on K Street from 7th to 14th streets was being converted into a pedestrian mall. This section included two of the city's finest old buildings, Weinstock's Department Store and the Cathedral of the Blessed Sacrament. The K Street Mall was officially dedicated in December 1969, 10 years after plans were originally conceptualized.

Perseverance also paid off for the backers of the Sacramento Convention Center five years later. Twice—in 1963 and 1966—voters had failed to give the necessary two-thirds majority to bond issues to build a community auditorium and exhibit hall at the east end of the K Street Mall. In 1968 the city and county formed a joint powers authority to issue bonds for the $20 million project. The 2,400-seat auditorium and the adjoining 50,000-square foot exhibit hall opened to rave reviews in June 1974. The *Bee* arts editor called the auditorium tops in acoustics and decor.

After the opening of the convention center, attention turned back to the west end of K Street. The section between 3rd and 7th, a continuation of the K Street Mall, was formally designated Downtown Plaza. It, too, was turned into a pedestrian mall, graced by fountains, waterways, and imaginative concrete sculptures.

When the K Street Mall opened in 1969, it was hailed as a concrete sign of progress—and almost immediately the public started complaining about the concrete. Some observers called the angular sculptures and waterways "a series of tank traps." Artists and architects countered that public taste was uneducated, but eventually people would learn to appreciate the abstract explorations of line, form, and texture characteristic of modern art.

Undaunted, the city in 1977 commissioned nationally known Sacramento artist Gerald Wahlberg to build an arch at the west end of K Street. When the design of the 40-foot, slightly tipsy steel arch was revealed, the *Union* opposed it and the *Bee* asked, "Is it art?" Nevertheless, the monumental structure entitled the Indo Arch was completed in May 1980. At the dedication ceremonies, billed as the "Festival of the Arch," the mayor and members of the City Arts Commission defended the monumental structure as an exciting work and proclaimed stoutly, "Public art is by its nature controversial."

However mixed its reception, the Indo Arch symbolized a public commitment to art. Soon three walls of the city parking lot in the west end boasted colorful murals and enameled copper mosaics, all commissioned by the city.

Two blocks south of K Street, Capitol Avenue (formerly M Street) was also the focus of redevelopment efforts following World War II. Here the problem lay in presenting a fitting approach to the seat of government and the capital city. Many visitors, entering the city from the west, formed their

At the turn of the century when this photograph was taken much of the area around the Capitol was still residential. At that time almost all state business was conducted in the Capitol. During the 1920s the State began to expand its facilities, and the buildings at the right in this photograph were replaced by the Library and Courts Building. Courtesy, Bidwell Mansion Collection, California Department of Parks and Recreation

Between 1953 and 1955 the State of California built several buildings, designed by Alfred Eichler, along the mall to provide additional office space. The Employment Development Building, shown here, spans two blocks on the south side of the street. The Sacramento Housing and Redevelopment Agency completed the rehabilitation of Capitol Avenue from the river to 9th Street. Courtesy, Ralph Shaw Collection, SMHD

The federal government contributed to Sacramento's revitalization. This eight-story federal office building, completed in 1961, attracted private developers to build on Capitol Mall. Among other functions, this building housed the federal courts. Courtesy, McCurry Collection, SMHD

first impression of the city as they drove over the M Street bridge and through the middle of the west-end slums lining both sides of Capitol Avenue. By the 1950s the city's front entryway looked dismally shabby.

The Capitol itself had been buffered from urban blight since 1928, when the state had built two Greek Revival-style buildings on Capitol Avenue directly in front of the Capitol Building. One housed various state offices, and the other housed the State Supreme Court and the State Library. A circular fountain later built between the two buildings gave an added touch of elegance.

Needing more office space, the state further buttressed the approach to its portals with three buildings immediately to the west of the two Greek Revival edifices. The Personnel Department and the Education Department each acquired a substantial structure on the north side of Capitol Avenue; and the Employment Development Department moved into a building which extended over two blocks on the avenue's south side. All three buildings were completed between 1953 and 1955.

Under the auspices of the Redevelopment Agency, the avenue was widened, and center strips were installed and planted with grass. Dilapidated buildings bordering the avenue on the west end were torn down. Finally, the street was given a new name: Capitol Mall.

As the appearance of the downtown area improved, developers who had been building in the suburbs began to look again at the central city. By 1981 a dozen private investors had announced the inception of major office projects.

As state government expanded in the years following the Second World War, the State became a prime downtown tenant. In 1978 the office of the Secretary of State pioneered a trend by moving into a renovated historical structure, the Public Market at 13th and J. The following year the State Department of Corrections moved into the refurbished J.C. Penney's department store on the K Street Mall.

By 1977 the State was leasing almost 2 million square feet of office space at 55 locations (about half in the downtown area). That year a master plan was adopted; and in 1981 the energy-efficient Bateson Building at 9th and P was completed.

Over a period of 30 years the federal redevelopment program and the state building program had pumped over $300 million into new and renovated buildings. Sacramento would never have been able to revitalize without such a huge infusion of money, but private investors also played an important part. Their contributions surpassed that of any government agency.

The combined efforts of city, county, state and federal agencies and private enterprise paid off in 1975, when a federal study of the quality of life in American cities ranked Sacramento near the top. In addition to economic indicators, the survey evaluated political, environmental, educational, and social well-being. Among the 65 metropolitan areas in the United States with a population of 500,000 or more, Sacramento, the city once known for having the worst slum west of Chicago, finished second.

Two new industries were becoming increasingly important in the late 1970s: tourism and electronics. By the 1980s the convention and tourist trade had stimulated thousands of new jobs in food services and lodgings. Both downtown and in the suburbs, new hotels were built and older ones renovated. Also by the 1980s almost all large computer manufacturers had sales and service offices in the metropolitan area, and many were seeking to develop manufacturing facilities in the Sacramento Valley.

While growth solved some problems, it created others. Freeways became

By the 1920s the west end of Sacramento was in a decline. Characterized by warehouses, cheap restaurants, lodging houses, and farm labor offices, the area continued to deteriorate until the urban revitalization programs began in the 1950s. Courtesy, C. Derrico Collection, SMHD

intolerably congested during rush hours. Bus service was excellent in some locations, spotty or nonexistent in others. The rails which used to carry street-cars and electric trains into the city had been torn up during World War II. But it seemed to many that a solution which had worked well in the past might be modified to meet the needs of the future. By 1982 the city and county had worked out comprehensive plans to develop a new light rail system.

By the 1980s Sacramentans had come to appreciate and respect their past, not only for practical solutions to problems, but also for its aesthetic and cultural legacy. But it was not always so.

In the 1950s the emphasis was on modernization. The earliest urban renewal projects started by tearing down old relics of the past. As the state freeway-building program accelerated, municipalities sought to kill two birds with one stone by planning freeway routes through their worst slum areas. Dilapidated buildings would then be torn down to make room for the new superhighway, thereby combining slum clearance with improved traffic flow.

Thus it came about that Sacramento's first preservation battle was fought over the location of a freeway.

In 1961 the State Highway Commission announced three alternative routes for Interstate 5, which would extend from Mexico to Canada. The new route could bypass Sacramento by following the west bank of the river on the Yolo County side; it could wipe out the embarcadero, the heart of Old Sacramento, by putting an elevated roadway over Front Street; or it could preserve a limited portion of the city's historic birthplace by cutting between 2nd and 3rd streets.

Sacramentans fought the second two proposals vehemently. On December 14, 1961, they packed the basement hearing room in the Public Works Building on N Street. Television cameras carried the highly-charged Highway Commission proceedings into homes and offices throughout the county.

Four years earlier the state had marked the Old Sacramento area for preservation. When the controversy heated up in 1961, the *Bee* urged the Highway Commission to weigh the consequences of the freeway routing decision: "It will affect the face of the capital city for generations; it will affect the business economy of the city for generations; it involves an historical heritage shared by the state and by the nation."

Despite public protest, the Highway Commission two years later adopted the 2nd and 3rd street route. Preservationists consoled themselves that at least the embarcadero had been saved, and perhaps the freeway would be useful in providing a distinctive boundary for the historic area.

The next major preservation battle developed about 10 years later on the east side. In 1972 plans were announced to turn the old Alhambra Theater, once known as a magnificent pleasure palace, into a supermarket. Concerned citizens circulated petitions, obtained a court injunction to delay the demolition, and raised a substantial amount of money—but not nearly enough to buy out the grocery chain. In 1973 voters turned down a bond issue to save the Alhambra.

When the wrecking crews tore the Alhambra down, they left a small wing standing on the parking lot's south side. Next to the remains of an ornate blue-tiled fountain, the leafy branches of a tree lay spread against the white stucco wall. Years after the Alhambra's demolition, a passerby climbed the steps to the fountain, lifted the branches, and found a bronze plaque, one of many which had once graced the courtyards of the palatial movie house. It bore an inscription from the 74th verse of Omar Khayyam's *Rubaiyat*, an epitaph for the palace and the age of romantic fantasy it symbolized:

This 1930 photograph shows the Alhambra movie palace on its third anniversary. In 1972 the theater became the focus of a battle between preservationists and developers. The Committee to Save the Alhambra failed to raise enough money to save the historic structure, so it was torn down to make way for a grocery store. Courtesy, California State Library Collection, SMHD

This 1938 photograph shows one of the fountains that graced the grounds of the Alhambra Theater. When the theater was demolished in 1972, one fountain was spared. On the south side of the parking lot at Alhambra and J, the fountain gives mute testimony to lost elegance. Courtesy, Sacramento City-County Library Collection, SMHD

The Junior League of Sacramento took on the reconstruction of the Eagle Theatre in Old Sacramento State Historic Park as one of their special projects. The League provided historical research, worked on the archaeological excavations, and raised funds for construction. The fund-raising performance of "Doin's at the Diggin's" was presented in the early 1970s. Courtesy, Norman L. Wilson

Yesterday this day's madness did prepare
To-morrow's silence, triumph, or despair
Drink! For you know not whence you came, nor why
Drink! For you know not why you go, nor where.

The fall of the Alhambra brought new recruits to the preservation cause. After lifting a glass and shedding a tear, preservationists regrouped, steadfast now in their aim to save the city's remaining historic treasures.

In 1973 the Sacramento Branch of the American Association of University Women published a guidebook, *Vanishing Victorians*, depicting some of the city's historic homes. Although some of the finest Victorian homes had already been lost, many remained, and the association urged their preservation as residences, offices, and business property. At the same time a newly formed homeowners group, the Sacramento Old City Association, organized its first annual Home Tour, putting several refurbished Victorians on display. In the next few years the homes in the central city skyrocketed in popularity, as young couples, singles, and retired people moved in with hammers, saws, and "how-to-do-it" books to bring new life to the once-proud dwellings.

Spurred by this grass roots activity, the city council in 1975 created the Sacramento Preservation Board to protect historic structures. The Board's expressed policy encouraged preservation, "not only as a means of retaining a valued and unique heritage, but as a technique for urban revitalization."

Following two years of study the Preservation Board in 1977 listed 583 structures in the central city as having historical, cultural, or architectural significance. A few property owners objected to being on the list because it prevented them from remodeling or removing their buildings as planned.

The historical renaissance created a new interest in Sacramento's three outstanding Victorian structures—the Crocker Art Museum, the Governor's Mansion, and the Stanford Home—which had survived, well-preserved, into the 1970s.

The city had taken over the care and maintenance of the Crocker Art Museum in 1885, when it was presented as a gift to the people by Margaret Crocker, widow of State Supreme Court Judge Edwin B. Crocker (counsel for the Central Pacific Railroad). The city appointed a nonprofit organization, the Crocker Art Museum Association, to manage it. Over the years the association expanded the museum, adding a new wing in 1969. The gallery was restored to its original Victorian colors and interior decor in 1979.

While the city maintained the Crocker Art Museum for the public, the state maintained the Gallatin mansion as a residence for its chief executive. The ornate Victorian Gothic home had been built in 1877 for Albert Gallatin, president of the Huntington and Hopkins Hardware firm. Beginning with Governor George Pardee in 1903 and ending with Governor Ronald Reagan in 1967, the mansion served as home for 13 governors and their families. After the Reagans moved out, the state parks department opened the home for public tours. On special occasions historians and community volunteers presented dramatizations of life in the mansion's early days.

After serving for more than half a century as a children's home, the historic Stanford Home at 8th and N became a part of the state park system in 1978. Leland Stanford, governor of California and president of the Central Pacific Railroad, had bought the home in 1861 and remodeled it during the 1870s, raising it from a two-story to a three-story building. His wife, Jane, bequeathed the house to the Catholic diocese, which set up an orphanage and later turned it into a home for disturbed children. As a historic state park site, the Stanford Home will be refurbished and opened to the public.

While individuals and families were moving back into the inner city and renovating Victorian homes, government agencies and private developers were rehabilitating Old Sacramento. Because of the impending Interstate 5 construction, little visible progress had been made in the 1960s, although state and local agencies did make plans and arrange for financing. In 1965 the area was declared a National Historic Landmark, and in 1966 Old Sacramento was placed on the newly-established National Register of Historic Places.

From 1965 to 1971, the Sacramento Redevelopment Agency busied itself with the acquisition of properties and the removal of tenants on the 28-acre site between the I Street bridge and Capitol Mall. A few hardy pioneers had already begun rebuilding. In 1961 the Cope family had restored the Firehouse Restaurant, originally built in 1853 to house the volunteer fire department. For a decade it remained an anomaly—a high class restaurant attracting well-to-do clientele and politicians into the west end slum. The Redevelopment Agency in 1970 completed the Morse Building (which presently houses the Visitors' Center), owned a hundred years previously by Dr. John Morse, pioneer physician and chronicler of Sacramento history. In 1970 the Big Four Building—so named after the four promoters of the Central Pacific Railroad—was moved from its original location to a site near the planned Railroad Museum at Front and I.

Between 1974 and 1977, some 26 prominent structures were completed—more in 1976, the Bicentennial year, than any other. State-sponsored projects included the restoration of the B.F. Hastings building, which had been the Wells Fargo office and later the western terminus of the Pony Express, and the reconstruction of the Central Pacific Passenger Station on Front Street. The Sacramento Junior League recreated the Old Eagle Theater of '49er days, while private developers refurbished the Railroad Exchange building on Front Street. Soon the wooden sidewalks and cobblestone streets were bustling with activity as visitors wandered among attractive shops, a one-room schoolhouse, restaurants, and professional offices.

The state helped finance several other major historical projects. From the mid-1970s to the early 1980s it made improvements at Sutter's Fort and the Indian Museum, built a multimillion-dollar Railroad Museum, and reconstructed the historic State Capitol.

The California Department of Parks and Recreation sponsors Living History Programs to foster interest in local history. The programs are held several times a year at the Governor's Mansion, the Central Pacific Railroad Depot, and Sutter's Fort. Participants, like this laundress at Sutter's Fort, play their roles by taking on the clothing and speech of a historical character. Courtesy, Judy Stammerjohan

Historic preservation in Sacramento began with Sutter's Fort in 1891. The Native Sons and Daughters of the Golden West rebuilt the neglected structure. This turn of the century photo shows the restored fort still surrounded by fields. The fort is now a unit of the California State Park System. Courtesy, David Joslyn Collection, SMHD

During the late 1970s, scaffolding, ladders, and metal bracing were familiar sights at the State Capitol Restoration Project. One of the largest restoration projects ever undertaken, it cost over $60 million dollars. The six-year project began in 1976 and was completed in January 1982. Courtesy, *Elk Grove Citizen* photograph by db Malloy

Sutter's Fort was one of the state's earliest restoration projects. After the Gold Rush the fort was used for a variety of purposes (even as a hog farm), and by 1891, when the state first undertook to preserve the historic site, the outer walls had crumbled and the adobe building was falling apart. Together with the Native Sons and Native Daughters of the Golden West, the state rebuilt the fort to preserve the spirit of John Augustus Sutter's New Helvetia. In 1940 the state built the Indian Museum, on the north side of the grounds of the fort.

In May 1981 the Old Sacramento waterfront became the scene of one of the largest collections of historic railroad equipment ever assembled, as locomotives from around the world arrived to help California celebrate Railfair '81, the grand opening of the State Railroad Museum. The three-story brick museum housed 21 fully restored locomotives, freight cars, and passenger cars amidst a variety of exhibits telling the story of railroading. One year after its opening, the museum had hosted more than 800,000 visitors, outranked in attendance in the state park system only by the Hearst Castle at San Simeon.

In 1982 the celebration of the state's heritage shifted to the heart of the city, the State Capitol itself. Like the original construction of the Capitol, the reconstruction had taken twice as long and cost twice as much as anticipated. The six-year, $68 million project entailed removing the entire interior of the building while keeping the exterior intact. Over 3,000 skilled artisans were employed to restore the building, inside and out, to its turn-of-the-century elegance.

At the opening day ceremonies on January 9, 1982, State Senator James Mills likened the stately white edifice to the great cathedrals of Europe. The *Union* called it "an eye-dazzler," and the *Bee* described it as "an ennobling, hallowed structure." But perhaps the comment that best captured the reaction of the general public was that given by one visitor to the day's festivities, who said with an expression of reverence, "It's the beautifullest thing I've seen in my whole life."

While the state sponsored the Capitol restoration and the Railroad

Museum construction, hundreds of individuals and community groups took on smaller-scale projects. As part of the grass roots historical revival, Sacramento County citizens restored a one-room schoolhouse, dug up a brothel-owner's past, and re-created on film the memory of a dual-culture farming community.

The Rhoads School, a one-room schoolhouse on the property of Myrtle and Ralph Murphy, which had served families in the south part of the county from 1872 to 1946, was given by Murphy descendents to Sacramento County. After it was placed on its new foundation in Elk Grove Park in 1976, local students and community members chipped paint, sanded desks, and repainted inside and out. It became a "Living History" museum, as modern-day teachers brought their classes to the schoolhouse to go back in time, having them recite lessons from McGuffy's readers and teaching them to bow and curtsy.

"Some of the newest and most advanced educational theories were practiced of necessity in these old-fashioned schools," said one of the educators, herself a former student in the Rhoads School. "The one-room school stands as a monument to the intense desire for education felt by our pioneer forebears."

Another grass roots project involved getting down to earth with trowels and whiskbrooms, and uncovering clues to everyday life in a brothel. Backed by the Los Rios Community College District and Cosumnes River College, two archeology instructors in 1978 secured permission from the owners of a to-be-restored hotel in Old Sacramento to do an archeological excavation in the basement. The one-semester project turned into a four-year enterprise, involving more than 60 students and community volunteers.

They unearthed wine bottles, fragments of china, combs, hairpins, toothpaste holders, perfume bottles, cold cream jars, and a $5 gold piece. Two other buildings had been on the site also—a tinsmith shop and another brothel.

While archeologists were literally digging into the past, a history professor and members of two ethnic associations were retrieving a community story with notepads, tape recorders, and slide projectors. From the early 1900s until 1942, two peoples from widely divergent cultural backgrounds created a

The ghost of the Gold Rush returned to Sacramento in May of 1922 during the "Days of '49" celebration. An entire gold camp rose on the sand lot on I Street that was occupied by the Southern Pacific Depot a few years later. A mountain highlighted the area's transformation. Courtesy, California Department of Parks and Recreation Collection, McCurry Photograph, SMHD

community characterized by interracial friendship and respect for each other's cultural heritage. Portuguese and Japanese families had settled on small family farms in the Freeport-Pocket district south of Sacramento. There they worked, played, and went to school together until the Japanese were evacuated during World War II.

In 1982 members of the Portuguese Historical and Cultural Society and the Japanese American Citizens League combined resources with California State University, Sacramento, and produced a multimedia documentary, "Strange and Wonderful Harvest." The documentary, a slide show with taped narration, has been shown to university audiences and community groups.

While students, professionals, and community volunteers did historical research, the city and county planned a museum to preserve the history of the valley. Ground was broken in November 1982 for a $4.8 million History Center next to the Railroad Museum in Old Sacramento. The History Center will house interpretive displays covering the history of the Sacramento Valley from the days of the earliest Indian settlements to the present. It will chronicle the ongoing development of the heart of the Golden State—the Sacramento Valley and its people.

Throughout its history, the city and county of Sacramento have reflected the actions and aspirations of many people since the Swiss adventurer, John Sutter, landed on the shore of the American River in 1839. Today's opportunities are different, but no less challenging, than those of the past. The same qualities of aggressive leadership, courage and perseverance in the face of natural obstacles and human imperfections which were exhibited in the past are still in evidence today, and will be needed in the future. These qualities may be found both in individuals and in their organizations—the businesses, government agencies, and non-profit associations—working together to make Sacramento one of the Golden State's most desirable areas in which to work and live.

Sacramentans have long been conscious of their unique place in California's history. The formation of the Sacramento Pioneer Society in 1850 demonstrates the venerability of this awareness. This photo shows Gold Rush costumes worn at the May 1922 "Days of '49" celebration. Courtesy, David Joslyn Collection, SMHD

Sacramento grew on a low plain at the confluence of the American and Sacramento rivers. During the 1850s and 1860s the city was periodically subjected to severe flooding. This lithograph shows the intersection of Front and J streets during the flood of January 1850. The accuracy of this Casilear and Bainbridge print enabled renovators to authentically reconstruct several historic buildings. (SMHD)

During the fall of 1848, Captain C.A.M. Taber sailed his vessel up the Sacramento River. Like many sailors he sketched and painted the places he visited. This is the earliest known view of Sutter's embarcadero, as it was called then. (SMHD)

Sacramentans took pride in the benefits of cheap electricity. As shown in this rather romantic postcard view, electricity enabled stores to stay open and streetcars to run well after the moon came out. Courtesy, Donald Napoli

Below the confluence with the American River, the Sacramento River flows westward through the flourishing fields of the Sacramento Valley. The river then becomes the Sacramento-San Joaquin Delta and empties into San Francisco Bay. Photo by Shirley M. Burman

Sacramento's red sandstone post office building was a well-known landmark at the corner of 7th and K streets. Built late in the 19th century the building stood until it fell victim to post-World War II development. Courtesy, Donald Napoli

This American-class locomotive, built by the Cooke Locomotive and Machine Works in 1888, was restored by Short Line Enterprises, Inc. The locomotive is currently on display at the California State Railroad Museum in Sacramento. Photo by Shirley M. Burman

The folk group "Golden Bough" performed at this craft show in Folsom in 1981. The gas-lit Sutter Street Mall has been closed off occasionally for pedestrian activities such as craft, art, and antique fairs. Photo by Shirley M. Burman

This child savors a cracker during the dedication ceremony of Indian Grinding State Historic Park in 1975. The park features a Miwok village with cedar bark dwellings and a ceremonial round house. The Kit Carson Mountain Men and Miwok families participated in the dedication. Photo by Shirley M. Burman

This log milling operation is located east of Grass Valley on the Colfax Highway. Photo by Shirley M. Burman

Storage silos gleam in the early morning light on a farm outside of Sacramento. These silos collect the bounty of the Central Valley before it is shipped to market. Photo by Shirley M. Burman

The California State Fair often highlights the state's cultural diversity. Here a group performs a Mexican dance at the 1981 fair. Photo by Shirley M. Burman

Objects can stir a memory. The man peering into the firebox of this old steam tractor could be recalling driving a similar vehicle. This photograph was taken at the Vintage Gas Engines and Tractor Show at the 1981 California State Fair. Photo by Shirley M. Burman

Facing page: The Folsom Lake State Recreation Area, located outside of Sacramento, has facilities for all water sports. This colorful Hobie Cat Regatta is an annual event. Photo by Shirley M. Burman

California's State Capitol was completed in 1874. Many of the structure's original features were recently restored during a $66 million facelift. Photo by Shirley M. Burman

The restoration of California's State Capitol took six years and cost $66 million. The inside of the dome reveals the work of the many craftspeople who participated in the project. Photo by Shirley M. Burman

The California Exposition and State Fair complex features a minirail transportation system, seen here at dusk. Photo by Shirley M. Burman

Bruce Beasley's cast acrylic sculpture, "The Apolyman," highlights the space between the Twin Towers state office buildings. Photo by Shirley M. Burman

These water fountains, outside the Plaza Towers, provide visual and aural refreshment to passersby. They are part of the urban open space provided by the Capitol Mall. Photo by Shirley M. Burman

Left and bottom: The E.B. Crocker Art Museum is the oldest art museum in the west. Dating from 1870, the house features magnificent parquet floors and beautiful inlaid ceilings as well as its prominent collection. Photo by Shirley M. Burman

The Governor's Mansion, a state historical landmark since 1968, was the home for 13 governors between 1903 and 1967. The Victorian Gothic mansion was built in 1878 for Albert Gallatin, a Sacramento hardware merchant. Photo by Shirley M. Burman

The Jazz Jubilee fills Old Sacramento with music each Memorial Day weekend. Photo by Shirley M. Burman

As part of her visit to the United States, Queen Elizabeth II of England toured Sutter's Fort on March 4, 1983. Courtesy, California Department of Parks and Recreation. Photo by Shirley M. Burman

This unprepossessing log structure helped launch one of the greatest migrations in American history. On January 24, 1848, millwright James Marshall saw a glittering stone in the mill's tailrace. The reconstructed mill is now part of the California State Park System. Photo by Shirley M. Burman

Ghosts of the '49ers still haunt the foothills of the Tuolumne County gold country. Early morning tule fog casts a sepia light over the scene. Photo by Shirley M. Burman

The California State Flower, the California poppy, can be seen growing throughout the Golden State from early spring through late summer. The California poppy thrives on the long summer and the semiarid climate. Photo by Shirley M. Burman

Left and below: Much of the area surrounding Sacramento retains its bucolic beauty. The agriculture of California is a staple of the state's economy. Photo by Shirley M. Burman

The advent of inexpensive electrical power extended Sacramento's business day after sunset. Stores, restaurants, theaters, and public transportation all expanded their operating hours. Electricity also favored the growth of manufacturing in Sacramento. This 1930s photo shows K Street looking west from 10th Street. Courtesy, David Joslyn Collection, SMHD

Chapter 8

PARTNERS IN PROGRESS

Sacramento's business community has provided leadership in all facets of community life since the time of the city's founding. Its two daily newspapers have roots going back to the Gold Rush days. Some of its business establishments have been in the same family for as many as four generations.

Today the largest single industry is government, employing over one-third of the metropolitan area's work force. The private sector is an ever-changing kaleidoscope of thousands of small businesses and hundreds of large ones, providing the goods and services that people want.

Because Sacramento, a political power center, has attracted many people of strong political orientations and individualistic personalities, controversy is a fact of life; but the underlying relationship between government, business, and the community at large is that of a dynamic and supportive interdependency. A healthy community attracts the workers and customers that business needs, and the taxpayers and voters to keep government going; a profit-making business sector provides jobs and creates a sound tax base; and an orderly government serves both business and the community at large.

The businesses and institutions whose stories are detailed more fully in the following pages have chosen to support this important literary and civic project. They illustrate the variety of ways in which individuals and organizations have contributed to the growth and development of the Valley. They range in size from a few employees to several thousand. One, a health services provider, has a strong volunteer component.

These partners in Sacramento's progress represent manufacturing, food processing, construction, wholesale and retail trade, professional services, and education. Some are nonprofit associations, some are sole proprietorships, and some are large corporations.

Besides providing high-quality goods and services, the partners share a tradition of working for community improvement. Many have organized professional and trade associations to improve skills and keep up-to-date on the latest products. They have supported civic organizations, charitable events, cultural activities, fine arts, and educational programs. The civic involvement of Sacramento's businesses, institutions, and government agencies, in partnership with its citizens, has made the city one of the better places to live.

We hope that you will enjoy meeting a few of the people, the companies, and the institutions that have helped build Sacramento.

Sacramento County Historical Society

Through poppies, plaques, programs, and publications, the Sacramento County Historical Society has endeavored for 30 years to cultivate the seeds of interest in local history.

"When we first started in the 1950s," recalled Joseph McGowan, founding president, "we were the only group here besides the Native Sons and Daughters who were organized for the preservation of the past."

The 47 charter members who met at the California State College in September 1953 included educators, book collectors, and a few members of long-established families. Guest speaker Judge Peter James Shields, age 92, told the gathering, "History is what men and women are doing all over the world and if we watch events we should see the direction we are going and how it will affect our lives."

As a living memorial to the western

The Sacramento County Historical Society annually sponsors and coordinates special events for Sacramento County History Week. The Living History Program at Sutter's Fort, organized by the California Department of Parks and Recreation, shown here, is a part of history week. (Courtesy of Norman L. Wilson.)

pioneers the Society in 1957 planted California poppies and blue lupine in the fields outside the city. The next year a number of youth groups and civic organizations joined in the effort, and soon the annual poppy-planting program became a statewide project.

In 1959 the Society moved its monthly meetings from the college campus to its present location at the Garden and Arts Center at McKinley Park. That same year, it launched a program of placing memorial plaques at historic sites, giving capsule histories of such events as the Pony Express, the Sacramento Valley Railroad, and the old Coloma stage road.

Throughout the 1960s the Society kept interest in local history alive through its public education programs, featuring speakers, a newsletter, *Golden Nuggets,* and a quarterly publication, *Golden Notes,* all of which are still going strong. Topics of monthly programs have ranged from a demonstration of '49ers' pans and shovels to a nostalgic slide show on picture postcards. *Golden Notes* has chronicled such topics as the explosion of the river steamer *Washoe,* the Volunteer Fire Department, the Chinese community of Locke, the

One of the primary programs of the Sacramento County Historical Society is publications. Here Dr. Joseph McGowan, its founder, looks over copies of *Golden Notes,* a quarterly publication of the Society. (Courtesy of *The Sacramento Union*—photo by Steve Yeater.)

governor's mansion, and, in 1983, the people who settled in the delta. In 1977 the Society published *Sketches of Old Sacramento,* a set of essays commemorating dramatic events such as the raising of the city streets.

The decade of the 1970s witnessed a grass-roots revival of interest in historic preservation, along with a proliferation of local organizations working together to inspire a renewed appreciation of the past. To honor individuals and groups who make outstanding contributions, the Society each December presents awards of merit.

By 1982 the August *History Week* had become an annual countywide social event, with the Historical Society coordinating historic displays, living history presentations, and other commemorative activities involving hundreds of individuals, associations, and businesses. The highlight of the week is the birthday celebration at Sutter's Fort, in which the call to refreshments is given by an authentic cannon salute.

Membership in the Sacramento County Historical Society is open to anyone interested in the history of the Sacramento area.

Crystal Cream and Butter Company

Crystal Cream and Butter Company today processes almost all of the milk produced in Sacramento, Solano, Sutter, Yolo, and Yuba counties—over 50 million gallons per year. The raw milk is purchased from 130 valley dairies, some milking as many as 4,000 cows a day. Crystal processes milk, cottage cheese, butter, yogurt, sour cream, and ice cream for distribution to 17 Northern California counties.

At the turn of the century many families kept one or two cows. They took their surplus milk to any of the numerous creameries in town to be churned into butter, which stayed fresh and usable much longer than milk. George Knox, manager of a creamery downriver at Clarksburg, started the Crystal Creamery at 11th and J in Sacramento in 1901. He expanded the business following the 1906 earthquake. Since many of the dairies in the Bay Area were disabled, Knox hired drivers and began shipping cream and butter to San Francisco. In 1913 he moved the business to its present location at 10th and D Street.

Celebrating its 51st year, Crystal sponsored a display at the California State Fair in 1952.

In 1901, the same year that Knox started Crystal, another dairyman, Carl F. Hansen, arrived in Humboldt County from Denmark. Born in 1876, he had attended the Danish Agricultural College, served a year in the Army, and worked in a Danish creamery. After he arrived in the United States he married Gerda Dahlquist, a native of Sweden, and they became the parents of three sons, C. Vernon, Kenneth, and Gerald.

When founder Knox died in 1921, Carl and Gerda Hansen purchased Crystal Creamery and moved to Sacramento. The boys helped out after school and on weekends making deliveries, moving cans and boxes, sweeping up, and learning the business. "If we wanted any allowance," Gerald later recalled, "we worked for it."

Crystal limited its products to cream and butter until the advent of refrigeration. Taking advantage of the new technology, Crystal provided Sacramento with its first bottled milk in 1931. As the company matured, so did the Hansen family. All three sons went to college, then returned to help manage the growing business. By the 1980s a third generation had assumed a leadership role in the family enterprise. Gerald's

Crystal maintained a fleet of Kleiber trucks, built in Oakland in the 1930s, to bring 10-gallon cans of milk from the farms to the creamery for processing.

son-in-law, Chuck Hills, who had joined the firm in 1972, was named vice-president and Don Hansen, Kenneth's son, became president in November 1982.

With Gerald Hansen still active as chairman of the board, the plant at 10th and D has become California's largest one-site milk-processing facility. Its subsidiary company, Sacramento Vitafreze Division, manufactures ice cream bars and frozen novelties. Additional distribution centers are located in Stockton, Concord, Yuba City, and Tahoe.

Crystal Cream and Butter has over 400 employees, many of whom have been with the firm for years. The people at Crystal take pride in their work, adhering to the highest standards to bring quality dairy products to consumers. In addition, they give freely of their time and energies to many varied community projects and activities to help provide a better life for Valley residents.

M.J. Brock & Sons, Inc. (Larchmont Homes)

The Sundial Plan: the first passive solar production home by M.J. Brock & Sons, Inc.

The Northern California division of M.J. Brock & Sons, Inc., pioneered affordable housing in the Valley in the 1950s and energy-efficient housing in the 1980s. Known in Sacramento as Larchmont Homes, the company has built over two dozen communities in the area, providing homes for about 12,500 families.

The firm's history dates back to 1922, when founder Milton J. Brock, Sr., began building custom homes in Southern California. As his sons grew to maturity, he brought them into the business. Milton Jr. became part of the company in 1938 and his brothers, Wendell and Carroll, joined a few years later.

To meet the postwar demand for housing, M.J. Brock & Sons, Inc., devised techniques for putting up large numbers of homes quickly, becoming one of the first companies to be both land developer and home builder. The new methods proved so successful that the Los Angeles-based organization soon directed its attention to another rapidly growing part of the state, the Sacramento Valley.

In 1952 the firm started construction on a large tract of land in North Highlands near McClellan Air Force Base. The development was tagged Larch-

mont Village in an informal tribute to the Larchmont Boulevard headquarters in Los Angeles, and the name Larchmont has identified Sacramento-area developments of M.J. Brock & Sons ever since. Within a few years Wendell and Carroll Brock moved to the area with their families to supervise the construction of a succession of Larchmont communities.

The sound financial position of M.J. Brock & Sons, Inc., was further enhanced when it was acquired by a major holding company, INA Corporation, in 1969, resulting in substantial growth. In 1982 INA merged with Connecticut General, resulting in a new parent company, CIGNA.

Milton Jr. took over the leadership of M.J. Brock & Sons, Inc., in 1972, following the death of the founder. While remaining chairman of the board, in 1976 he turned the presidency over to

Richard C. Chenoweth, an executive with many years of experience in the company, and the first president not related to the Brock family. Family involvement remains strong, however. One of the founder's grandsons, Ted Cox, is Los Angeles division manager. Another grandson, Steve Brock, serves as an independent consultant in marketing and advertising for the firm.

Carroll Brock became head of the Northern California division in 1967, after his brother Wendell died. He has continued the Brock tradition of building homes that are economical, yet meet high standards of quality and craftsmanship.

Under Carroll's leadership, Larchmont Homes pioneered the development of solar and energy-efficient housing subdivisions. The company designed and built the first production passive solar home, the "Sundial," in West Sacramento in 1980. This model earned the Suntherm Award from Pacific Gas & Electric for achieving better than 50-percent solar efficiency, and received commendations from the California State Energy Commission, the Pacific Coast Builders Conference, and the National Association of Home Builders. Larchmont plans to continue its leadership in energy-efficient, affordable housing in the greater Sacramento area.

This home is one offered at Larchmont Sunriver, one of the more recent and most luxurious Brock developments.

North Sacramento Land Company

When Carl E. Johnston graduated from college, he moved to the Sacramento Valley and started the development of the city of North Sacramento. Today the North Sacramento Land Company, which he cofounded over 70 years ago, has shifted from residential development to the building and leasing of commercial property, but it remains in the family and continues to play an important part in the community.

Carl's father, Daniel W. "D.W." Johnston, was a professional land developer of many years' experience at the time the Rancho del Paso, a Spanish land grant just north of the American River, was put up for sale. D.W. bought 4,400 acres in 1910 and incorporated the North Sacramento Land Company while Carl was still a student at Stanford University. D.W. turned the management of the firm over to Carl upon the young man's graduation.

After Carl moved to the new development site in 1913, he subdivided the land and put in streets and sewers. He organized water and power companies. He donated land for schools and parks and a Boy Scout camp. He crusaded for an electric streetcar through North Sacramento, between Sacramento and Roseville, to augment the three railroad lines already in service.

The North Sacramento Land Company advertised the merits of country living, "just nine minutes from Eighth and J with a five-cent commutation

An old North Sacramento Land Company advertisement, which appeared July 28 and 29, 1917.

fare." It featured shady oak groves and good soil, with alfalfa, fruits, and berries growing there. It was ideal for raising poultry. Between 1913 and 1916 the population of the area multiplied from 80 to nearly 1,600. By 1916 the company reported that the area had two schools, five stores, 300 homes, 10 miles of concrete and macadam highways, and 10 miles of water mains. That same year a concrete automobile bridge was built across the American River, further improving accessibility. During World War I, North Sacramento secured a government contract to build an airplane factory, the Liberty Iron Works,

which accelerated the area's growth.

With Johnston's continuing influence, North Sacramento by the 1920s had organized its own city hall, police station, fire department, schools, library, and other municipal services. After the flood of 1928, Johnston promoted the improvement of levees and permanent flood-control measures.

The family home was in the Woodlake district, one of the earlier Johnston developments. After Carl died in 1953, his wife Myrtle stepped in to continue the work. In 1954 the Johnstons' son-in-law, Robert J. Slobe, joined the firm to look after the insurance department. Myrtle utilized the large expanse of land just south of Highway 160 north of the American River to develop the Johnston Industrial Park. The Woodlake Inn is perhaps the most familiar landmark, but the area also includes offices, warehouses, and distribution centers for many businesses.

Since the Johnstons' daughter, Carolyn Slobe, took over management of the North Sacramento Land Company in 1971, she has continued to develop its holdings and to encourage commercial properties which feature attractive architecture, natural landscaping, and a concern for the total environment.

Today's headquarters of the North Sacramento Land Company is located at 400 Slobe Avenue, Sacramento.

McGeorge School of Law/University of the Pacific

The "courtroom of the future" is here today at McGeorge School of Law of the University of the Pacific in Sacramento. The circular chamber is furnished in muted earth tones of brown, rust, and gold, creating an air of calm dignity. Built-in videotaping equipment enables aspiring lawyers and their professors to review the proceedings. The courtroom has received national and international attention since it was built in 1973. It represents but one of many innovations and accomplishments that have contributed to McGeorge's reputation for excellence.

Before it developed a full-time program, McGeorge persevered as a part-time evening school for over 40 years. In 1921 a Sacramento lawyer, Verne Adrian McGeorge, and his wife, Annabel, held classes in their home for a small group of students, since the closest law school at the time was in San Francisco. In 1924 a group of community leaders joined with the McGeorges to found the Sacramento College of Law. Professor McGeorge was appointed Dean. Five students comprised the first graduating class. Verne Adrian McGeorge died in 1929; prior to that date the school's name had been changed to McGeorge College of Law. Annabel McGeorge continued to serve

as registrar until her retirement in 1958.

The law school moved to its present site in the Oak Park district of Sacramento in 1957, and Gordon D. Schaber, an attorney who had joined the faculty four years previously, was appointed Dean. There were at that time 123 students enrolled in the evening classes. Under Schaber's leadership the law school expanded its programs, campus, faculty, and enrollment. It opened a three-year, full-time day division in 1966, when it merged as the McGeorge School of Law with California's oldest university, the University of the Pacific in Stockton (founded 1851).

McGeorge pioneered a legal clinic in the 1960s to give law students practical experience and to provide economically deprived clients access to legal assistance. In 1969 it launched the *Pacific Law Journal*, a quarterly review devoted to scholarly analysis and in-depth reporting of California legislation.

Advanced studies were introduced in the 1970s, including a master's program in business and taxation law, foreign studies in Austria and Scotland, and internships in various European countries. McGeorge recently started a summer pre-law program for undergraduates considering a career in law.

As academic programs expanded,

Gordon D. Schaber, Dean and professor of law, has served as the presiding judge of the Sacramento County Superior Court, as chairperson of the City Planning Commission, and as chairperson of the ABA Section of Legal Education and Admissions to the Bar.

new buildings were added to the campus, including classrooms, an auditorium, faculty offices, residence halls, recreation center, student center, community legal services center, library additions, a center for advanced studies, and most recently, a 300-seat lecture and seminar complex for special programs and continuing legal education presentations. By 1982 the 17-acre campus included 26 buildings in an attractively landscaped setting which provides the most distinctive living and learning environment in American legal education.

The student body in 1982 numbered approximately 1,400, divided evenly between the full-time day and part-time evening programs. McGeorge in 1982 was awarded a Chapter of The Order of the Coif, the highest academic recognition which can be awarded to any of the 172 law schools accredited by the American Bar Association. McGeorge also holds membership in the Association of American Law Schools.

The circular "courtroom of the future" was first among the nation's law schools in 1973: a fully-operating model for testing new technology applicable to trial procedures and providing realistic advocacy training for future attorneys.

The Palm Iron and Bridge Works

Charles Palm used his artistic talent to make carriages and ornamental iron gates for Sacramento residents in 1886. Today the company he founded builds steel frameworks for multistory buildings throughout the western states.

Palm opened his first shop on Front Street, but moved to 11th and J and then to 6th and K before the turn of the century. In 1904 he moved the Carriage Works to a shop building out at 15th and S, which was so isolated that employees used to shoot wild ducks in the neighboring slough. There it remained for the next 78 years, even as it became surrounded by homes and light commercial activity.

With the advent of the automobile the demand for carriages decreased. Palm diversified in 1910 by making garbage wagons (still drawn by horses) for the city. In 1925 the firm fabricated and erected the steel framework for the 14-story Elks Temple at 11th and J, followed by the Forum Building and a Greek Revival-style bank building. It also fabricated and erected the steel for a six-story state office building in San Francisco.

Palm Iron fabricated and erected the framework for the 14-story Elks Temple at 11th and J, shown here under construction in 1925.

During this period, general manager Percy Reese entered into partnership with founder Palm. Throughout the 1940s and 1950s Palm's son, Gene, headed the company together with Reese's widow, Hilda. As the Reeses' daughters, Margaret and Jean, reached maturity, they, too, became involved in the venture.

When Margaret's husband, G.R. Messick, joined the firm in 1942, Palm Iron and Bridge Works was building ship bodies for Kaiser Liberty ships. "We used to put the sections on barges and float them down the river to the bay," Messick recalled.

Capitalizing on the postwar construction boom, Palm Iron supplied structural steel for schools and commercial buildings. Ironically, the "baby bust"—the lowered birth rate of the 1960s—provided impetus for further expansion. Colman Schwartz, Jean's husband, explained, "We used to have two or three schools going all the time and then schools just stopped. We knew we had to grow, or stay small and probably get extinguished."

Looking to the future, Palm Iron purchased a 24-acre site south of the city on Elder Creek Road in 1976 and began construction of a modern shop capable of handling virtually any project typical

Steel fabricated by Palm Iron supports many state office buildings, including this one at 8th and N, Sacramento, constructed in 1980. Many of the buildings in the background also contain Palm Iron substructures.

of the company's market area. The move to the new plant was completed in 1982, when all fabricating equipment was consolidated at the new site.

Continuing the tradition of family involvement, G.R. Messick is president, Colman Schwartz is secretary-treasurer, and their wives share in policy decisions as members of the board of directors. A younger generation has recently joined the ranks. Son Stephen Schwartz is executive vice-president and son Alan Messick is in production. Daughter Kristina Schwartz Rogers is a director and her husband, Gary Rogers, is a management representative. The firm employs over 150 shop workers and more than 45 people in the engineering and administrative departments.

"The key to our strong market position is versatility," a Palm Iron executive affirmed. "We can bid on a wide range of heavy structural steel projects, as well as the most intricate and sophisticated miscellaneous metal projects."

Emigh Hardware Store

Three generations of Emigh family members have shaped Sacramento's largest locally owned retail hardware store. The company now has 60 employees, many with 20 or 30 years of experience. In its 29 departments the firm stocks over 25,000 items for both homeowners and professionals.

Two brothers, James and Clay Emigh, founded the Sacramento store in 1910, but they had accrued a decade of hardware experience prior to that. James bought his first store in Suisun City in 1900. His younger brother, Clay, helped out in sales. In 1908 Clay moved to Sacramento. Two years later James sold the Suisun City store and opened a new business at 1208 J Street, with Clay in charge of sales. In 1912 the Emigh brothers merged with Winchell and Cline, added a line of agricultural implements and buggies, and moved to larger quarters at 310 J Street. In 1918 the Emigh-Winchell store moved back up J Street to Seventh, where it remained for the next 14 years, with James as president and Clay as a member of the board.

The president's twin sons, James Jr. and Albert, started working in the store about 1920. Their younger brother, Col-

by, joined them a few years later. When James retired in 1931, Clay became president, James Jr. and Albert both sat on the board of directors, and Colby was in sales. The next year, 1932, Clay also retired and the second generation took over. Albert and Colby moved Emigh's Hardware Store farther up J Street to the corner of 13th.

Attracted by the postwar building boom in the suburbs, Colby in 1952 supervised Emigh's move to the newly developed Country Club Center at El Camino and Watt. The newer, more mobile population had trouble pronouncing the name, so in the early 1960s the company introduced a cartoon character depicting a pigtailed girl in overalls saying, "Call me Amy." Little Amy, still a familiar feature in Emigh advertisements today, was a composite of Colby and Jesma Emigh's two daughters, Carol and Mary.

Emigh-Winchell's was located on J near Seventh throughout the 1920s. This picture, taken in 1922, indicates a shift in the product line, with paints and varnishes a specialty.

By 1973 the business had again outgrown its quarters, so it erected a modern 35,000-square-foot facility across the street from its old location, more than doubling its floor space. The new building at 3555 El Camino features exposed aggregate panels with natural wood accents and wood laminated beams, and landscaped parking areas in the front and back.

Emigh's stocks all kinds of goods for home and garden maintenance and remodeling projects, ranging from giftwares and pet supplies to bathtubs and potbellied stoves. Some of its departments are paints, garden, nursery, power equipment, sprinkler, electrical, housewares, patio, tools, and screen doors. Salespeople are trained to give expert advice on how-do-to-it projects.

Many family members have been actively involved in the store at various times. Carol's husband, William Welker, was employed from 1953 to 1964. Jeffrey, Laura, and Leslie Welker helped out after school and on weekends before they moved away. Now Brian and Stacey, the children of Richard and Mary Emigh Lawrence, are receiving an introduction to the business. Richard Lawrence, who began his career as an electrician, became general manager in 1971. When Lawrence became president of the company in 1980, he represented its third generation of family leadership.

Emigh's newest store, at 3555 El Camino, features over 25,000 items for the improvement, maintenance, and remodeling of homes and gardens.

The Sacramento Union

Nine striking printers set up their own newspaper, *The Sacramento Union*, in 1851 after the owners of two financially troubled papers cut expenses by reducing the printers' wages. The printers bought their own press, hired author-physician John J. Morse as editor, and opened shop in a tiny room on J Street between Front and Second.

The first issue rolled off the press on March 19, 1851. Soon mules were carrying *The Union* to all parts of the Mother Lode, where prospectors affectionately nicknamed it "the Miners' Bible."

The fledgling newspaper survived both flood and fire in the early years. After the flood of 1852, *The Union* led the move to rebuild the town and construct levees. On November 2 of that same year, fire swept through the city, destroying the newspaper office along with many others. Employees saved a small press and some type. The second

This is the original headquarters of *The Sacramento Union*, which is located in Old Town. It is part of the state's recent restoration of this historic section of Sacramento.

morning after the fire, *The Union* reappeared to tell the story.

A few weeks later *The Union* moved into a new brick building on J Street between Front and Second. In May 1853 the owners sold the paper to James Anthony, who brought the first steam press to the city. With steam power replacing the laborious hand-printing process, the paper expanded its daily, weekly, and steamer editions and added a semiannual pictorial edition.

During the 1850s *The Union* campaigned for the construction of the transcontinental railroad, but later opposed the monopolistic power of the Central Pacific. It continued its editorial opposition to the railroad interests until it was merged with the railroad-owned *Sacramento Record* in 1875. For the next 28 years it published under the name of *The Sacramento Record-Union*.

In 1903 Alfred Holman acquired the paper and it became once again *The Sacramento Union*. Following a succession of owners, Earl Craven and James Meredith bought it in 1921 and moved to 1910 Capitol Avenue.

While on a trip to the Sandwich Islands (now the Hawaiian Islands) Mark Twain was a contributor to *The Sacramento Union*.

The paper continued to change hands every few years until it was acquired by William Dodge in 1929. It remained in the Dodge family for 33 years, the longest single ownership in its history. A group of Sacramento investors purchased it from the Dodge estate in 1962.

The La Jolla-based Copley Newspapers bought the paper in 1966. With Copley's backing, *The Union* in 1968 built its present headquarters at 301 Capitol Mall, adding a revolutionary technological innovation: a four-story-high Goss Metro offset press capable of printing 60,000 papers an hour.

Copley Newspapers sold *The Union* in 1974 to John P. McGoff, president of a Midwest publishing group, who in turn sold one-half of his interest in 1977 to Richard M. Scaife. In 1982 Scaife acquired full ownership and assumed the position of publisher and chairman of the board. Under his stewardship the oldest daily in the West will continue its ongoing programs of expansion and improvement which have led *The Sacramento Union* to be one of the largest morning newspapers in California.

The Thomson-Diggs Company

The Thomson-Diggs Company is the only full-line wholesaler of hardware in the Valley, delivering goods to several thousand independent retail outlets in Central and Northern California, southern Oregon, and western Nevada.

The founder, Frederick "F.F." Thomson, came to Sacramento from Vermont in 1872. After teaching school for a few years, he entered the hardware business with the San Francisco firm of Frank Brothers. In 1878 he was commissioned to open a branch store at the corner of Second and J, Sacramento. Several years later F.F.'s brother Herbert joined the firm, which by then was known as Stanton-Thomson Company. On January 5, 1900, the Thomson brothers merged with the Diggs Implement Company, which had moved to Sacramento from Woodland two years previously, and became incorporated as

Today's headquarters of The Thomson-Diggs Company.

The Thomson-Diggs Company became the first corporation chartered by the state of California in the 20th century. This photograph shows the Second and J location in 1900.

The Thomson-Diggs Company—the first corporation chartered by the state of California in the 20th century.

The wholesale hardware company moved in 1911 from J Street to a new four-story warehouse at Third and R streets, historic site of the first passenger terminal for the Sacramento Valley Railroad in 1855.

In 1932 Thomson-Diggs extended its historical roots back to the Gold Rush by acquiring the Schaw-Batcher Company, direct descendant of the Huntington, Hopkins & Company Hardware Store. This venture was established in 1849 by two of the men who later built the Central Pacific Railroad, Collis P. Huntington and Mark Hopkins.

When Thomson-Diggs was incorporated in 1900, F.F. Thomson served as its

first president. He was followed by Marshall Diggs, C.F. Prentiss, and John W. Geeslin. A second generation took over with the accession of the founder's son, F.F. Thomson, Jr., and later Charles L. Mason, son of the founder's daughter. The current president and general manager, Edward S. Towne, started working for the organization in the early 1950s and became president in 1971.

Over the years the product line has shifted as a result of new technologies. At the turn of the century the business stocked buggies, wagons, and plows. The advent of the gasoline engine phased out horses, so the firm increased its selection of shelf hardware and home products. Although nuts and bolts remain a staple of the business, the home center concept has taken hold. Thomson-Diggs provides thousands of items for home maintenance, gardening, and sports.

The company has enlarged its quarters several times since 1911. Today it has 270,000 square feet of warehouses and office space located on one and three-quarter blocks between Second and Fourth, R and S streets, near the center of downtown Sacramento. Prompt deliveries are facilitated by its location next to the interchange and crossing of Interstate 5 and Interstate 80, the transportation hub of Central and Northern California. The facility includes 640 feet of rail siding and 50,000 square feet of customer and employee parking. Besides the staff at headquarters, Thomson-Diggs has 28 field representatives to service its accounts in California, Oregon, and Nevada.

Aerojet-General Corporation

Rocket engines and motors made in the Sacramento Valley help scientists explore the far reaches of the universe.

Aerojet-General Corporation, a pioneer in defense and aerospace technology, builds a wide variety of rocket systems in its Sacramento complex just south of Highway 50 near Folsom. Aerojet today consists of five companies, two in Southern California and three in Sacramento County. Aerojet is a wholly owned subsidiary of General Tire &

Aerojet's Orbital Maneuvering Subsystem engines performed successfully on five space shuttle flights to date.

Azusa to the Sacramento Valley, where a large expanse of barren land made an ideal testing site—remote, yet close to the metropolitan area. At one point Aerojet owned more than 20,000 acres. Its present site covers a more modest, but still substantial 8,500 acres.

After the Russians launched Sputnik in 1957, the United States poured huge

A U.S. Navy Standard Missile is being launched from a surface ship.

Peacekeeper Stage II motor systems like this one are designed, built, and tested at Aerojet.

Today, ready to meet the challenges of the 1980s, Aerojet's three Sacramento-based companies employ more than 3,200 people in all phases of liquid and solid rocket research and production.

Aerojet Liquid Rocket Company

The world's foremost producer of storable liquid propellant rocket systems, the Aerojet Liquid Rocket Company is now finishing up its historic association with intercontinental ballistics missiles, while continuing to build a variety of relatively small engines.

One of its best-known products is the Orbital Maneuvering Subsystem (OMS) used in the space shuttle program. The OMS engines provide orbit insertion, accurate maneuvering during space flight, and reentry from orbit. The reusable OMS engines are designed for 100 missions with a service life of 10 years.

Aerojet Strategic Propulsion Company

Aerojet Strategic Propulsion Company designs, produces, and tests large solid propellant rocket motor systems. Presently engaged in developmental work on the Peacekeeper missile system, it also remanufactures motors and provides engineering services for Minuteman and Polaris systems built in the 1960s and 1970s.

In addition to its defense work, the Aerojet Strategic Propulsion Company is applying aerospace technology to cancer research.

Rubber Company.

Aerojet was founded at the beginning of World War II in response to a challenge: the need to get military aircraft into the air from short runways. Dr. Theodore von Karman, a professor of aerodynamics at the California Institute of Technology, and several associates formed Aerojet on March 20, 1942, to build the world's first Jet-Assist Take-Off Rockets.

In 1951 Aerojet expanded from

sums into defense and aerospace to close the "Missile Gap." Aerojet employment zoomed up to 22,000 in the mid-1960s. By the end of the decade the United States had a network of missiles in place and man had walked on the moon. Abruptly, funding was discontinued, and by 1974 employment was reduced to 2,154. Despite its drastically reduced scale of operations, the company held on. By 1975 employment had stabilized. Aerojet has expanded gradually and steadily since.

Aerojet Tactical Systems Company

Over the years Aerojet Tactical Systems Company has built rocket motors for more than 10,000 Navy Standard Missiles and over 35,000 Army HAWK motors, in addition to a variety of solid propulsion systems for other tactical missiles.

Using advanced electronic technology throughout all phases of the assembly process, it employs 600 people in the most modern tactical rocket motor production facility of its kind in the world.

Martyr & Curry

Martyr & Curry is the Sacramento area's largest independent family-owned supplier of stationery and office equipment. Seven retail outlets offer a wide variety of accounting forms, legal and engineering supplies, electronic data-processing materials, furniture, exclusive gifts, engraved invitations, business machines, and office necessities. Owner and president Harry Curry directs all operations from a new 23,000-square-foot distribution center and corporate headquarters at 320 Commerce Circle.

The original business was established in 1946 at 914 J Street by Carl Martyr and his son, Leland. It later moved to 1024 J Street. A suburban branch was added in 1952 at 2721 Fulton Avenue.

Harry Curry attended and was graduated from the University of Santa Clara, after a four-year tour of duty with the Marine Corps during World War II. After attending Hastings Law School in San Francisco, Harry met and married the former Ilene Fries, and entered the retail field on a training program in department store management. This

A large oak tree shades Martyr & Curry's new distribution center, built in 1980, at 320 Commerce Circle, Sacramento.
Harry Curry, owner and president (right), and his son David, district manager, share the family's involvement in business and community concerns.

entailed traveling through various Northern California cities before making Sacramento their home in 1956, with their young daughter, Nancy, and their son, David, who was born in 1958.

In 1961 Harry Curry became a co-owner of the then-Martyr & Shine operation, and the name was changed to Martyr & Curry. Three years later the company opened a third store, at 4742 Manzanita Avenue.

Curry bought Leland Martyr's interest in 1967, becoming sole stockholder and chief executive. Continuing a tradition of steady growth, he opened a store in 1972 at 7225 Florin Mall Drive, and four years later another one at 537 Downtown Plaza. The corporation built its new distribution center and administrative headquarters in 1980. In the fall of 1982 Martyr & Curry added a seventh location in the Mills Shopping Center in Rancho Cordova.

Following in his father's footsteps, David Curry, recently graduated from Santa Clara University, now serves as district manager for the firm. Their daughter, Nancy, worked in the business until she married and began a family.

For the Curry family, running a business is just one part of a total commitment to community service. As a past president, officer, and member in the Sacramento Downtown Retail Merchants' Association and as a mem-

Martyr & Curry's oldest office supply store has been at the same location, 1024 J Street, for over 25 years. This picture was taken in 1961.

ber in the Rotary Club of Sacramento, Harry Curry has devoted many years toward civic improvement. He also serves on the Mercy Hospital board of governors and on the parish council of St. Anthony's Church. He was on the board of directors of the original Bank of Sacramento and organized Sacramento's third Small Business Investment Company. He has also been active in the Camellia Festival Association, the South Hills Racquet Club, Valley Hi Country Club, Del Paso Country Club, Serra Club, Big Brothers, and Grace Day Home.

Ilene Curry is a member of the Cancer League Society, past president and member of St. Patrick's Home Guild, member of Loyola Guild, past member of Mercy Guild, and a past member of the board of governors of the American Cancer Society.

Together with their children, the Currys have been involved in many youth activities, including YMCA, YWCA, Boy Scouts, CYO, Jesuit High School, and Holy Spirit School. David Curry is an active member of 20-30, and past president of Downtown Plaza Retail Merchants' Association.

Harry summed up the family's philosophy recently. "Service is the keynote to everything," he said. "The community has been good to us, and we, in return, want to be good to the community."

Hobrecht's Lighting

Hobrecht's Lighting has brightened up the Sacramento area for more than 70 years. Now with three retail outlets, it gives homeowners and contractors a wide selection of lighting fixtures. Among its specialties are Oriental lamps, crystal chandeliers, traditional lighting of polished brass and antique brass, ceiling fans, track lighting with interchangeable heads, and accessories to fit any decor.

When the Pauls bought Hobrecht's in 1972, it already had a reputation for quality and service dating back to 1909, when the company's founder, Joseph C. Hobrecht, opened a small shop at 1012 10th Street. His brother Philip soon joined him, and they made and sold all kinds of electrical equipment. In 1911 the J.C. Hobrecht Company designed and installed 465 ornamental electroliers—streetlights—for the city. Some may still be seen in Old Sacramento. The company also put up the original light standards lining the historic streets of Folsom. It has done the lighting for many public buildings, including Memorial Auditorium, and for many of the area's churches.

The Paul family acquired Hobrecht's Lighting in 1972. Shown here are (left to right) son Eric V.; Carolyn M., president; T. Stan; and daughter Karen E.

In 1929 Philip and his wife Maria moved the J.C. Hobrecht Company to a shop at 1912 I Street, where they ran the business together while raising eight children. One of their sons, John P. (Jack), joined the firm in 1946. Philip retired in the mid-1950s and Jack took over until November 1, 1972, when he sold it to another pioneering Sacramento family, the Pauls.

Carolyn Paul's grandfather came to Sacramento in a covered wagon as a little boy. He became an electrical contractor and did the lighting for many Sacramento churches. Stan's grandparents came west in a covered wagon, also, and settled in the Bay Area. Stan has been a general contractor in Sacramento for many years.

Running the business is a family project, and the Pauls' children, Eric and Karen, both help out after school and on weekends. The family travels together to markets in San Francisco, Dallas, Chicago, and New York to examine new products and bring back the finest selection for their clientele.

Two of Hobrecht's 12 employees have over 40 years' experience with the ven-

In 1911 J.C. Hobrecht designed these streetlights located in front of the original store. These lights are now being used in Sacramento's Town and Country Village and in Folsom.

ture. Both Sylvia Livingstone and Eugene Lofing started with the Hobrecht family and have stayed on with the Pauls. Lofing is in charge of the repairs department, which is noted for its efficiency in repairing all kinds of light fixtures.

The company has been at its present midtown location at 2311 J Street, Sacramento, since 1936. The Pauls opened a Hobrecht's Lighting at the Granite Bay Shopping Center in Roseville in 1981, and recently added a store for the convenience of eastern residents on Macy Plaza Drive in the Sunrise area.

Serving the customers is a team effort on the part of all Hobrecht's employees. "One of the most challenging and pleasurable aspects of this business," said president Carolyn Paul, "is helping our customers locate just the right fixture for the particular purpose in mind."

A. Teichert & Son, Inc.

From cellar floors to superhighways, A. Teichert & Son, Inc., has provided a rock foundation for the growth of the Sacramento Valley.

The company has three major divisions. The Construction Division builds roads, freeways, underground utilities, canals, bridges, dams, parking lots, and playgrounds. The Aggregates Division produces gravel, sand, asphaltic and ready-mix concrete, and precast items. The Land Company develops building sites and leases land and buildings.

The venture started as a small family business in 1887. Adolph Teichert, a German immigrant, was foreman for the California Artificial Stone Paving Company. He came to Sacramento to place sidewalks around the new state capitol. In the course of this work he met and married a Sacramentan, Carrie Knaul. In his first advertisement he called himself "a manufacturer of artificial stone for sidewalks, garden walks, carriage drives, stable and cellar floors, fencing, coping, etc." Cement for this work came by ship in barrels from Belgium.

The founder's son, Adolph Jr., graduated with a degree in engineering from the University of California. He became a partner in 1912. Through his influence, the company took on larger, more complex jobs. Father and son worked together for the next 30 years. Together they helped organize the Northern California Chapter of the Associated General Contractors in 1915, and both participated in many civic and charitable activities.

To counter the effects of the Depression, the firm set up a gravel plant at Perkins and introduced the use of ready-mix trucks. During the 1940s Teichert paved airfields and built revetments at Mather, McClellan, and Stockton Air Force bases. It built dams in California, Oregon, and Nebraska, worked on the Central Valley Water Project and, locally, did construction for Sacramento State University, the Port of Sacramento, and many residential and commercial projects.

Adolph Teichert, Jr., had three sons, all connected with the business—Adolph III, Frederick, and Henry. Henry is now chairman of the board and Lou Riggs, a son-in-law, is president. Fred Teichert and Jud Riggs, great-grandsons of the company's founder, are also active in A. Teichert & Son, Inc. Many workers have given 20, 30, or 40 years of service and several are second-generation employees.

The company has changed over the years to keep pace with technological advances and complexities. It has developed imaginative ways to preserve resources, control air and noise pollution, and to be a good neighbor.

Today A. Teichert & Son, Inc., employs about 200 full-time people and 800 seasonal workers. It provides construction work and aggregates products to Northern and Central California. With headquarters in Sacramento on the beautifully landscaped site of a reclaimed gravel plant, it also has district offices in Sacramento, Stockton, and Woodland, plus a sub-area office at Lake Tahoe. Teichert materials and labor have been responsible for a good share of the building of the Sacramento Valley.

Adolph Teichert, Sr., founder of A. Teichert & Son, Inc.

Adolph Teichert, Jr., joined his father's firm in 1912.

Gerlinger Motor Parts, Inc.

Gerlinger Motor Parts, Inc., rebuilds engines and machinery for trucks, railroads, farm equipment, food processing, elevators, printing presses, nuclear generators, and industrial and diesel engines, as well as private automobiles.

"Oftentimes one of our rebuilt engines will last longer than a brand-new one," president John A. Biggers stated, "because the metal has been heated and cooled, making it stronger and tougher; and we make sure that each piece matches the original specifications before we put it back together."

In addition to its precision machine shop, Gerlinger's features hard chrome and nickel plating, industrial and automotive parts, and hydraulic components. As parts jobber and warehouse distributor, Gerlinger's serves truckers

In 1940 Gerlinger Motor Parts, Inc., was located at 1424 J Street.

within a 150-mile radius, catering to owner-operators as well as fleets. Other customers include utilities, canneries and food processing plants, Bay Area Rapid Transit (BART), Amtrak, and Southern Pacific, aerospace industries, and various government agencies throughout Northern California.

The machine shop and sales office are located just about a mile east of the state capitol, at 2020 K Street, with a separate warehouse nearby. The company was founded April 1, 1940, by a former railroad machinist, George Gerlinger, and his wife Ella, office and credit manager. John Biggers joined the firm in 1944 as a counter clerk right out of high

John A. Biggers, president and general manager, has been with Gerlinger's since 1944.

school. "In those days," he recalled, "Gerlinger Motor Parts was basically only in the parts business with a small machine shop, and over the years we have added equipment so that now we can handle almost any vehicle or industrial part."

In 1959 Biggers bought a part interest and became a vice-president of the company. When the Gerlingers retired in 1967, he became the controlling stockholder and president. A disastrous fire in 1976 almost wiped out the firm, but with the help of employees, suppliers, local businesses, the insurance company, and sympathetic competitors, Gerlinger's was back at work with an improvised sales counter the very next

afternoon, and had the shop facilities rebuilt within five months.

Today the firm has 34 employees, including several members of the second generation of the Biggers family: daughter Marlene, sons Calvin and Curt, and son-in-law Ron Mencarini (whose father, Frank Mencarini, is vice-president in charge of sales orders and traffic and has been with the organization for many years).

Biggers was founding president of the Industrial Education Council, an area-wide effort to provide hands-on vocational experiences for students and to improve communications between educators and industry. He has been active in Boy Scouts, YMCA, Sacramento Safety Council, and Rotary International, has served on advisory bodies to Sacramento City College and the Los Rios Community College District, and is listed in several national and international publications. John Biggers and his wife Esther recently incorporated the Biggers Charitable and Philanthropic Foundation, chartered nationally under the Heritage Foundation of Virginia, to provide funds for educational purposes and medical research.

This photo of the Gerlinger Motor Parts facility and employees was taken in 1955. It is still at this location—2020 K Street. Ella M. and George A. Gerlinger, founder of the firm, are at the right. Frank Mencarini, vice-president and assistant store manager, and John A. Biggers are 13th and 16th from the left, respectively.

Weinstock's Department Store

Since its founding in Sacramento more than a century ago, Weinstock's Department Store has pioneered new ideas in merchandising and in services to the community. The company's elegant replica of a Paris department store at 12th and K was a downtown landmark for over 50 years. Now the new flagship store at Sixth and K heralds the revitalization of the K Street Mall, while four more stores dominate regional shopping centers. In addition, Weinstock's has three stores in the San Joaquin Valley, one in Nevada, and three in Utah.

The firm's founder, David Lubin, traveled around California mining camps playing his violin and delivering merchandise for several years before starting a store in San Francisco in 1872. He brought a supply of men's clothing and dry goods to Sacramento in 1874 and, with financing from his sister, opened a small shop at Fourth and K.

Soon his younger half-brother, Harris Weinstock, joined him.

At that time merchants usually haggled with their customers over the price of goods. Lubin introduced a novel concept: one fixed price, plainly marked on the goods, and cash only. "I can assure you I had a tough time," Lubin later recalled, "but I ran things according to my idea of what was right and stuck to them: fixed prices marked in plain figures, and no lying as to the quality of the goods."

Within 20 years the brothers had expanded the one-room shanty into a lofty, spacious building with a gleaming white exterior and a full line of fashions

---

In 1924 Weinstock-Lubin & Co. opened this department store at 12th and K in downtown Sacramento. Modeled after a famous Parisian store, it offered many unique services and innovations to its customers.

and furnishings. A contemporary reporter described the brothers' personnel policies as "peculiar, if not eccentric" in their attention to the welfare of their 300 employees. They provided a lunchroom and kitchen for employees, started a library, and, in an early version of work-study programs, gave classes on company time and at company expense for those employees who were not yet 18 years of age.

Lubin retired from Weinstock-Lubin & Co. in the 1890s to pursue a project to relieve world hunger by improving crops and distribution methods. He organized the International Institute of Agriculture in Rome, which later became the United Nations Food and Agriculture Organization.

Weinstock remained active in the store until 1908, when he was appointed state labor commissioner and traveled around the world to study labor conditions. Three of the founders'

sons, Simon and Jess Lubin and Robert Weinstock, became leaders of the company and guided it into the 1920s.

In 1903 a fire destroyed the white building and all of its contents. The next day employees set up makeshift quarters at the Old Pavilion, Sixth and M, and opened for business with merchandise coming in from the freight station. Undaunted by disaster, the company built a newer and finer store at the original location, with a grand opening just one year later.

As the city grew, the business district moved eastward. The firm drew up plans for a building that would remain the center of the district for many years to come. In 1924 hundreds of Sacramentans gathered to celebrate the completion of the new store at 12th and K. Modeled after the famous Printemps department store in Paris, the three-story reinforced concrete structure featured columns and facings of cream-colored terra-cotta tile, with a high archway marking the K Street entrance. The interior design was spacious, with the latest in lighting and ventilation, noiseless elevators, drinking fountains, and a complete sprinkler system to protect against fire.

Among other innovations, the corporation paid the train fare for customers from neighboring towns, provided a child care center for shoppers, and sponsored a traveling fashion show. It brought seminars, cultural exhibits, and art shows to Sacramento.

Weinstock-Lubin became a subsidiary of Hale's in 1926, but it continued its tradition of local management and community involvement. During World War II the firm helped maintain morale on the home front by educating consumers in the use of substitute materials and supporting war loans and welfare drives through advertising and displays.

In 1951 the parent corporation, Hale's, merged with the Broadway Department Stores to become Broadway-Hale Stores, which later became Carter Hawley Hale Stores. Later the Hale's stores at Ninth and K and at Arden Fair merged with Weinstock's.

Located in the Downtown Plaza, the new headquarters and flagship store is accented dramatically on the L Street side by this 55-foot-high Romanesque arch.

Weinstock's operated two downtown stores within three blocks of each other until 1976, when the Ninth and K store was closed preparatory to consolidation of the downtown facilities in a newer, larger store in the middle of the mall.

With the expansion of suburbs, Weinstock's led the way in the regional shopping centers. It opened branch stores at Country Club Plaza and Arden Fair in the north area in 1961, at Florin Center to the south in 1967, and at Sunrise Mall in 1972.

In the 1960s and 1970s Weinstock's expanded into the San Joaquin Valley—one store each in Stockton, Modesto, and Fresno—and into Reno, Nevada. Late into the 1970s it acquired a store in Murray, Utah, and built stores in Salt Lake City and Ogden.

The new headquarters and flagship store in the Downtown Plaza, Sixth and K, opened in 1979. The three-level building of steel and concrete is accented dramatically on the L Street side by a 55-foot-high Romanesque arch, which is repeated in a smaller form on the K Street Mall side. The interior combines dramatic flair with practicality,

arranged to provide the utmost in customer convenience.

Weinstock's stores feature the latest in women's, men's, and children's fashions and decorative home furnishings and accessories. They specialize in presenting high-quality, trend-setting merchandise gathered by their own buyers throughout the United States and abroad. They also offer a variety of services, special events, and demonstrations designed to appeal to customers' needs and lifestyles.

They have won numerous awards for their support of the arts and cultural and charitable activities in their communities. They have been strong supporters of the Sacramento Symphony, the Open Ring Art Gallery, and the Tempo Gallery in the Crocker Art Museum. Weinstock's is one of the few department stores in the country with its own permanent art collection.

Diepenbrock, Wulff, Plant & Hannegan

The founder of Sacramento's oldest law firm argued and won the state's first environmental lawsuit in the 1880s. Today the firm of Diepenbrock, Wulff, Plant & Hannegan is one of Sacramento's largest law firms, with 17 partners and 19 associates providing a full range of legal services.

The founder, George Cadwallader, arrived in Sacramento with the early-day gold miners. In 1855 he opened a law office in Bennett's Masonic Hall on J Street between Front and Second. Five years later he took on an apprentice, Robert T. Devlin, who soon became a partner in the firm. In 1881 Cadwallader assisted the state attorney general in the precedent-setting environmental suit, *People of California* v. *Gold Run Ditch and Mining Company*. After steamboat captains and farmers testified that hydraulic mining debris was ruining rivers and farmland in the Valley, the courts granted an injunction, and hydraulic mining soon ended.

Robert Devlin brought his brother William into the firm after Cadwallader retired, renaming it Devlin & Devlin in 1891. A.I. Diepenbrock and Horace B. Wulff joined the Devlins in the 1920s and in 1931 the firm left its offices at Fourth and J and moved into a high-rise office building at 10th and J. Shortly thereafter, William's son Arthur and A.I.'s brother Victor joined the firm.

A new generation came aboard during the 1950s, as Forrest A. Plant, John and James Diepenbrock, and Robert Wulff joined the firm. Two more partners were added in the 1960s: Cyrus Johnson and John Hannegan.

In 1967 the law firm became one of the first tenants in the new office complex at 455 Capitol Mall. Twelve more partners were added in the 1970s and 1980s. John Gilmore contributed exper-

tise in litigation and hospital law; Thomas "Tac" Craven, probate; Peter Doyle, litigation; David Riegels, antitrust matters; William Sumner, taxation; and Dennis Murphy, labor law. Dennis Campos and James Freeman added strength in the field of business law, Douglas T. Foster in communications, while William Shubb, Jack Lovell, and John Fischer contributed skills in litigation.

The 1983 legal staff also included associate attorneys Charity Kenyon, Gregory J. Hughes, Karen O. Ahern, Brian T. Regan, Pamela A. Underwood, Robert L. Gallaway, Forrest A. Plant, Jr., Raymond M. Cadei, Timothy K. Roake, Thomas G. Mouzes, James C. Connelly, Michelle E. Bach, Francis M. Goldsberry, Edmund K. Brehl, Keith McBride, Jeff Owensby, and Timothy Murphy.

Diepenbrock, Wulff, Plant & Hannegan has represented businesses, government agencies, nonprofit organizations, and individuals in legal matters ranging from simple wills up to litigation and highly complex business transactions involving hundreds of millions of dollars. Some lawyers specialize in the taxation, probate, labor relations, communications, business or insurance departments, while others engage in a more diverse practice and draw upon the resources available within individual departments. The firm's own library is one of the largest private law libraries in Northern California. Diepenbrock, Wulff, Plant & Hannegan's attorneys also work with the County Bar Association to provide legal assistance to people who otherwise could not afford legal representation.

Partners in the firm of Diepenbrock, Wulff, Plant & Hannegan are (left to right, first row) Jack V. Lovell, John V. Diepenbrock, John J. Hannegan, Forrest A. Plant; (left to right, second row) Thomas A. "Tac" Craven, Cyrus A. Johnson, Robert R. Wulff; (left to right, third row) Peter M. Doyle, William W. Sumner, R. James Diepenbrock, David A. Riegels, William B. Shubb, John S. Gilmore, Dennis M. Campos, John E. Fischer, James T. Freeman. Not shown is Dennis R. Murphy.

RJB Company

The RJB Company has spearheaded the revitalization of downtown, the development of suburban business/industrial centers, and the bringing of high-technology industries to the Sacramento Valley. It is one of Sacramento's largest commercial and industrial real estate development firms. Its owners, the Benvenutis, have been responsible for the sale and leasing of over eight million square feet of commercial, industrial, and office space over the past 30 years.

RJB's influence in the downtown area may be seen in the renovation of existing offices, such as the historic Elks Building, and the construction of new offices for state agencies and private enterprise. In the suburbs RJB has built business/industrial parks at such diverse locations as Mather, McClellan, Sunrise, Northgate, and Westgate. It has worked closely over the years with the Sacramento Area Commerce and Trade Organization (SACTO) to bring environmentally compatible, high-technology firms to the area, and developed the Placer Center in Roseville, where Shugart manufactures floppy discs and accessories for computers.

Joseph Benvenuti, father of RJB's president and vice-president, came to Sacramento with his young family in 1949, leaving behind a career in the grocery business in New Jersey. Shortly after his arrival he entered the real estate field, first building houses and then commercial structures. He also started a building supply business.

Joe Benvenuti's sons, Richard and Gary, shared their father's enthusiasm. "My dad has always been the type of person who works literally every waking hour of the day," Richard recalled, "so it was hard growing up not to be influenced and interested in what he was doing."

After receiving his college education at California State University, Sacramento, Richard joined his father and another developer, Marvin "Buzz" Oates, in forming the RJB Company—the initials standing for Richard, Joe, and Buzz. The Benvenutis subsequently

bought out Buzz, and after graduating from the University of California at Berkeley, Gary "Bud" Benvenuti joined the firm.

In conjunction with their development activities, the Benvenutis have maintained a full construction staff. During the 1960s they built many tilt-up warehouses, so named because the concrete walls are tilted into place. These buildings provide quick, economical, utilitarian space for offices, storage, and distribution centers.

In the 1970s RJB shifted toward more emphasis on architectural distinctiveness and aesthetic qualities. The firm's clients have included restaurants, retail stores, wholesalers, manufacturers, food processors, fire departments, public utilities, and county and state agencies.

In the 1980s RJB emphasis has turned

Richard Benvenuti, president of the RJB Company.

to multistory office buildings and high-technology business parks. Many RJB projects currently are being done in partnership with other companies, such as Sacramento Savings & Loan; Capital Bank of Commerce; Interland Corporation of San Mateo; the Lewis Trust Group of London, England; and Cadillac-Fairview, a Canadian development firm. Today Richard Benvenuti is the president and general manager of RJB, his brother Gary is vice-president, and their father serves as consultant, while engaging in his own enterprises as well. As individuals and business owners, the Benvenutis take pride in contributing to Sacramento's future.

Simms Hardware Company, Inc.

Simms Hardware Company, specializing in guns and shooting accessories, has the distinction of being in the same location and under the same family ownership since its founding over 50 years ago.

B.G. Simms entered a partnership with Jim White of the White Hardware Company in 1924. Within a few months Simms bought out White and changed the name to Simms Hardware Company. The slogan, "Why go downtown; it's easy to park at 28th & J," was adopted. One local banker predicted that the business could not succeed so far from the downtown area.

Merle Simms, B.G.'s wife, did the bookkeeping for the store while raising

Simms Hardware has an underground range for test-firing repaired guns.

three children. All three youngsters worked in the store occasionally while still in school. When son Frank reached the age of 12, he began working on a regular basis. "I worked two hours a day, five days a week, for one dollar," Frank, now president, recalled. "Many of my young friends would have liked a job like mine."

After completing three and one-half years of wartime duty as a Seabee shooting instructor, Frank joined his father full time in 1946. In 1953 he married the former Thelma Johnson. Their son, David, who is now working in the business, was born in 1957.

Simms Hardware Company's original gun selection was displayed in a seven-foot-long glass cabinet and about half of the guns were B.G. Simms' per-

sonal property. His lifelong hobby of rifle marksmanship took him to national competition from 1918 on and he was one of a four-man team that set a national record score in 1951. With this shooting knowledge, B.G. Simms became a pioneer in the promotion of ammunition reloading and use of rifle scopes in the area. Frank Simms also shot in competition for many years. His top honors were as a member of the California State Rifle Team at the national competition, where he placed eighth in .30-caliber bolt-action aggregate.

B.G. Simms rode for the Pony Express in 1961—not the original, of course, but the centennial reenactment—taking the leg from Sutter's Fort (just a block from the store) to Perkins. He also has spent much time with state legislators on behalf of sensible gun regulation. *Sporting Goods Dealer Magazine* in 1970 awarded Simms Hardware its No. 1 Firearms Retailer Award for distinguished service to the industry.

In 1966 B.G. and Frank again expanded their store and built an underground range, a 27-inch tube 50-yards long for test-firing repaired guns or for sighting in.

Continuing a family tradition of involvement in the business community, Frank has served as board member and president of the California Retail Hardware Association, whose 600 members are dedicated to providing high-quality service and effective management.

The interior of Simms Hardware Company, showing its extensive stock of firearms.

Today Simms Hardware conducts about 70 percent of its business in gun-related items or service and about 30 percent in hardware. In addition to retail sales, Simms distributes shooting supplies to many smaller independent dealers and has a mail-order parts business that covers all 50 states. It is the oldest Colt warranty station and parts distributor in the country. Parts are also carried for about 70 other manufacturers. The Simms family has felt fortunate to combine a hobby with their business. The opportunity to own beautifully crafted guns, even if only for a short time, is very rewarding.

Frank Simms (left) and B.G. Simms (right), presenting a shotgun to California's Governor Ronald Reagan.

Wind Gap Gallery of Fine Art

Wind Gap Gallery of Fine Art, the "oldest" tenant in Old Sacramento's recently restored Mechanics' Exchange Building (118 I Street, located directly across from the California State Railroad Museum) is one of the finest on the West Coast. It opened in July 1977, four years before the completed construction and 1981 opening of the Railroad Museum.

Owner-Director of Wind Gap Gallery, Leafy Mayhew (former Director of San Diego Art Institute, Balboa Park, San Diego, California) regards herself as a pioneer in the development of the north end of Old Sacramento and points with pride to the fact that hers is the only business on I Street, in that section of the project, to have survived the turbulent construction period of the Railroad Museum and the fluctuating situations that have faced the restoration project because of an uncertain national economy.

Wind Gap Gallery presents both Western and traditional art works, which include the dynamic paintings of Western artist Anthony Sinclair; Americana watercolors by Stanislaus J. Sowinski; nature-oriented oils by Carl Zimmerman; Western oils by Dan Toigo; Chinese watercolors and silk scrolls by Kwan Y. Jung and Yee Wah Jung; and Americana bronzes ("Backbone of America" series) by Malcolm Alexander (recently commissioned by eight major oil companies to execute a 21-foot, half-million-dollar bronze sculpture in Valdez, Alaska, to pay tribute to the workers of the Transcontinental Pipeline).

In addition, the gallery presents the highly prized early Western bronzes of E.E. Heikka (1910-1941), who was a protege of C.M. Russell. (At the time of his untimely death, Heikka had completed 200 masterpiece clay sculptures, which were acquired by knowledgeable collectors who recognized the artist's great genius during his lifetime. Small, limited editions are being cast, for the first time, by the collectors of the original clay models, which now rest in the Cowboy Hall of Fame or in other well-known Western museums.) With the exception of Heikka, all artists represented at Wind Gap Gallery are California residents; however, they exhibit their works in important galleries throughout the country.

Coinciding with the 1981 opening of the Railroad Museum, Wind Gap Gallery presented a special historical exhibition of 28 original watercolor and oil paintings by Archie T. Newsom (1894-1978), nationally known architect, artist, historian, and Chief of the Architectural Section, U.S. Army Corps of Engineers. The art works depict early train scenes and familiar landmark buildings of Old

Sacramento and the Mother Lode country—buildings which Newsom diligently sought to have preserved for posterity. Several of these historical paintings, which belong to the collection of Mrs. Archie Newsom, may still be seen at Wind Gap Gallery, where they add an important dimension to the historical authenticity of the Old Sacramento restoration.

Director Leafy Mayhew devotes a large share of her time and efforts to giving daily lecture tours to her large visiting public, which comes from all over the world. In addition to advertising in national publications, she designs and prints most of her own public relations material, which visitors are eager to take

Leafy Mayhew presents "Old West" sculptures by Heikka and paintings by noted American artists in the Wind Gap Gallery of Fine Art in Old Sacramento.

back to their states or countries with information about Wind Gap Gallery and the Old Sacramento Restoration Project.

In addition to owning and directing her own business, Leafy Mayhew (who has a lifetime history of being a civic and cultural leader wherever she has lived) is a member of the Sacramento Metropolitan Chamber of Commerce; Sacramento City and County Historical Society; Friends of Sacramento History Center; Sacramento Visitors' and Convention Bureau; Old Sacramento Citizens' and Merchants' Association; P.E.O. Sisterhood, Chapter PQ; Crocker

Art Museum Association; and Western Alliance of Art Administrators. Her broad knowledge in the field of Fine Arts, her many travel experiences from living abroad for four years and visiting in 17 countries (including Russia), and her years of experience in the business world combine admirably to equip Leafy Mayhew to fill her present role as Owner-Director of her outstanding art gallery, which is a very important addition, not only to Old Sacramento, but to the entire city of Sacramento.

WEMCO

WEMCO, originally named Western Machinery Company, is part of the worldwide Baker International Corporation. WEMCO products are used throughout the United States and around the world. WEMCO manufactures pumps, oil/water separators, and processing equipment for fluid-waste handling, wastewater treatment, and minerals recovery.

WEMCO pumps handle everything from delicate food products to abrasive sludge in sewage treatment plants. WEMCO oil/water separators remove oily wastes from production water in oil fields, refineries, and other industries.

WEMCO materials-processing equipment is indispensable in the recovery and upgrading of coal, copper, iron, and other minerals.

The enterprise was founded in 1915 in Salt Lake City, when Harry N. How set up a shop to repair, rent, and sell machinery to mining companies and farm contractors. In 1917 How established a branch in San Francisco, and in 1923 moved the headquarters to that city.

The firm began to build its own line of equipment for processing gold ores in the early 1930s, responding to the demand for minerals processing equip-

ment which had resulted from the increased valuation of gold. Besides furnishing equipment, Western Machinery also designed and erected plants for mining operators. In 1934 the company established a plant and warehouse in Sacramento for convenient access to the gold fields.

In the 1940s Harry How's son, Jack, joined the business, which continued to expand. In 1955 it moved its Sacramento plant to the site of its present facility at 721 North B Street, and introduced the recessed-impeller vortex pump, designed to permit the pumping of solids and fibrous materials without clogging. These pumps are standard equipment in practically every sewage treatment plant in the country.

The Hows sold the organization in 1961 to the international engineering-contracting firm of Arthur G. McKee & Company, headquartered in Cleveland. The WEMCO Division moved its headquarters from San Francisco to Sacramento in 1965. Three years later WEMCO developed a unique rotor/stator for its flotation cells, which helped the firm become the world's largest supplier of these units to the mining industry.

In 1970 WEMCO was acquired by Envirotech Corporation of Menlo Park, specializing in wastewater treatment, air-quality control, minerals, and mining equipment. Under Envirotech's ownership, sales volume increased fourfold and WEMCO was able to significantly modernize its manufacturing capability by installing state-of-the-art automated machine tools as well as a computerized inventory management system.

Baker International Corporation acquired Envirotech in 1982; WEMCO was placed in the Baker Mining Equipment Company group. Today WEMCO has several facilities in Europe, in addition to its Sacramento headquarters. WEMCO expects continuing increases in sales volume throughout its worldwide markets as corporate researchers continually seek new ways of improving their products.

The interior of WEMCO's manufacturing plant as it looked 25 years ago (top) and as it is today. Note the overhead cranes and forklifts. A bank of electronic controls now regulates the fabrication of pumps and industrial processing equipment.

Bel Air Markets

A young couple from China started out as sharecroppers in America. Their children grew up to become the owners of a chain of supermarkets.

When Gim and Lee Shee Wong arrived in California with their five-year-old son in 1922, they worked as sharecroppers in Placer County. Gim's father, Yuen D. Wong, had come to the United States in 1868, and had returned to China to marry and raise a family. When he came back in 1914, 14-year-old Gim came with him. Two years later Gim and his father returned to China, where the parents had arranged a match, as was the custom, with a young woman from a neighboring village. Gim returned to America and worked five years to save enough to bring his wife and son over. Soon another son was born, followed by eight more sons and daughters.

In 1932 the Wongs took their small savings and bought five acres of rock-studded land in Penryn, where they planted fruit trees and vegetables. Gim bought a used truck and installed sides that opened out to serve as a mobile vegetable stand.

"We sold our produce door to door

Mr. and Mrs. Gim Wong, cofounders of Bel Air Markets, emigrated from China in 1914 and worked as sharecroppers in Placer County. In 1932 they farmed and sold produce door to door and in 1955, with their older children, opened the first Bel Air Market.

in Auburn," recalled George Wong, third son and now the president of Bel Air Markets. "Our father drove the truck, and we weighed and bagged the vegetables and fruit for the customers."

The three oldest brothers—Bill, Gene, and George—all served in the Armed Forces during World War II, then went into separate businesses. As the supermarket concept was beginning to catch on in the early 1950s, they held a family conference with Dad and Mom, brothers Albert and Paul, and sister Lillie. The Wongs opened their first Bel Air market in the newly developing south area, at Fruitridge and 63rd Street, in 1955. Two years later they opened a store in the northeastern suburbs at Arden and Eastern, followed by one at Dewey and Madison.

Bill took charge of the vegetables, going to the San Francisco produce markets at 2 a.m. (prime time for pro-

duce) twice a week to select the finest and load it onto trucks for morning deliveries to the Sacramento stores. Albert and Lillie managed the meat departments for many years. Gene served as financial advisor. Paul took on the maintenance of the truck fleet and the remodeling of the buildings. George, as president, has directed the overall course of the company from the beginning.

After the original store burned down in 1971, the Wongs rebuilt it, adding a bakery and a floral department. Expansion continued in the 1970s with a new headquarters at 1901 Royal Oaks Drive, another supermarket in the south area, one in Fair Oaks, and one in Elk Grove.

By 1982 there were six Bel Air stores in the Valley, with over 500 employees. Other administrative personnel include Rich Konkel, director of operations; John Combs, controller; Fred Hartup, advertising; and Nancy Beach, personnel.

Bel Air emphasizes customer service. "Many of our loyal customers have been shopping at Bel Air for years," said president Wong. "We look for opportunities to show our appreciation."

The Sacramento Bee

Four generations of the McClatchy family have carried on the journalistic ideals expressed in the first issue of *The Daily Bee* over 125 years ago: political independence and the pursuit of "a just, honorable, and fearless course of conduct."

James McClatchy came to Sacramento with the '49ers. He worked on the *Placer Times*, Sacramento's first newspaper, as well as several others before joining *The Bee* as a reporter when it was founded in 1857. He became an editor and part owner, spending 26 years with the paper. His son, Charles Kenny (C.K.), devoted 60 years to *The Bee*. C.K.'s daughter Eleanor headed the company for more than 40 years. Another C.K.—Eleanor's nephew, son of her brother Carlos and grandson of the first C.K.—has been president since 1978.

The original *Bee* building was on Third Street between J and K. In 1866 the paper moved to a building on the corner of Third and J. In 1880 the original building was remodeled and *The Bee* moved back into it, adding a steam-driven, double-cylinder press.

The full legal ownership of *The Bee* came to the McClatchy family in early 1884, shortly after James' death. C.K., who had been working with his father for the previous eight years, became editor and his older brother Valentine became publisher and business manager.

At the turn of the century *The Bee* moved into a new office at 911 Seventh Street, where it remained for the next 50 years.

C.K.'s son Carlos joined the staff in 1911. He inspired the venture's geographical expansion and its entry into the new field of radio. The McClatchys started *The Fresno Bee* in 1922 and acquired *The Modesto News Herald* in 1927, which became *The Modesto Bee* five years later. They invested in Sacramento's first radio station, KVQ, in 1922.

After Carlos, the heir apparent, died unexpectedly in 1933 and his father died three years later, the responsibility for continuing the organization fell to C.K.'s daughter, Eleanor. Although she was in New York studying to be a playwright, she returned to Sacramento to carry on her father's ideals: that the McClatchy newspapers continue to be "real tribunes of the people, always fighting for the right; to be fair to all; to decide questions by the light of principle, never under the slavery of petty or partisan politics."

Eleanor guided *The Bee* for the next 44 years. She was the primary force in taking the firm into television and in the founding and development of the Sacra-

mento Civic Theater, now known as the Eleanor McClatchy Performing Arts Center, and the Music Circus. In 1978 she went from president to chairperson of the board and her nephew, C.K. McClatchy, was named president. When Eleanor died in 1980, C.K.'s older brother James succeeded her as chairperson.

In 1953 the company moved into its present headquarters at 21st and Q. With its new press, *The Bee* added color photos. In 1959 it put out its first Sunday morning edition. Twelve years later it switched the Saturday edition from afternoon to morning, and in 1978 its weekday editions went morning also.

The Bee in 1981 completed a new production plant, representing an investment of more than $40 million in modern equipment. With a staff of nearly 1,000, *The Bee* is one of Sacramento's largest private employers.

Reflecting on *The Bee's* continuing goals, president C.K. McClatchy recently affirmed, "The greatest challenge is and will remain exactly what it was when this paper was founded in 1857: to gather and print the news honestly, fairly, and accurately, and in the process, to maintain the independence *The Bee* has now enjoyed for a century and a quarter."

Founded in 1857, *The Bee* was originally located on Third Street between J and K streets.

The Sacramento Bee, now at 21st and Q streets, is one of Sacramento's largest private employers.

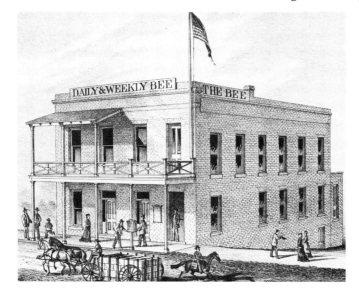

California Almond Growers Exchange

The California Almond Growers Exchange, headquartered at Sacramento, processes one-third of the world's crop of almonds—over 200 million pounds per year. Once a small specialty crop sold only at Christmastime, the almond industry has grown spectacularly. In the past decade acreage has doubled and tonnage has tripled. Today over 5,000 growers cooperatively own the California Almond Growers Exchange. Through the company they market their crop to all 50 states and 88 foreign countries.

processing plant in 1920. As bakers, confectioners, and homemakers discovered the convenience of shelled almonds, the Exchange in 1922 installed shelling and grading equipment.

The Exchange helped growers improve their cultural practices for better productivity. By 1940 more than 2,000 growers had joined, and the plant was processing 8,000 tons of almonds per year. Volume increased during World War II to supply the Armed Forces.

Growth accelerated during the 1950s

The first California Almond Growers Exchange plant (above) was built in 1914 beside the Western Pacific tracks. Six years later a five-story concrete building (below) was constructed right over it.

Early automation—women sorted almonds on a moving belt in the 1920s.

At the turn of the century growers sold their crops to independent dealers, negotiating individually on price. Dissatisfied with their treatment at the hands of these independent buyers, a group of 230 growers joined together in 1910 to form their own organization. They hired professionals to run it, and each grower-owner was paid according to the amount of almonds produced.

The Exchange built a small receiving and packing plant at 18th and C in Sacramento in 1914. That same year it introduced the Blue Diamond® label, printed on the burlap bags in which the nuts were packed.

The firm erected a five-story concrete

and the Exchange built concrete storage bins, cold-storage facilities, and automated equipment. In 1960 it installed electronic sorting machines and expanded its cooking and packing facilities. Through national advertising it sparked interest in almond recipes.

The California Almond Growers Exchange launched a worldwide campaign in 1955, appointing sales agents in Canada, Mexico, South America, Europe, Africa, and Asia. When it persuaded airlines to carry foil packets of Smokehouse® Almonds, passengers from all countries began to ask where they could obtain them.

While the marketing division opened up vast new territories, the research division developed new uses for the

product. Tasters, nutritionists, and scientists analyzed every aspect of the nut and nut products. They discovered that almond oil is rich in Vitamin E and may be used as the base for cosmetics, soaps, and pharmaceutical products.

As the world's largest almond-processing organization, the Exchange has facilities that include processing plants at Sacramento, Salida (near Modesto), and Fullerton, California; eight receiving stations located throughout the almond-producing areas of the Sacramento and San Joaquin valleys; and seven Almond Plaza® gift stores filling retail and direct mail orders. In addition, it has a branch office in Japan and a network of broker representatives in every major almond market in the world.

Plant facilities in Sacramento include 20 buildings for such functions as administration, research, processing, distribution, and storage. The headquarters remains at the original location, 18th and C, along with an Almond Plaza®. Another Almond Plaza® is located in Old Sacramento. Processing is in full swing for about eight months of the year. With over 2,000 employees during the peak of its season, California Almond Growers Exchange is Sacramento's second largest private industrial employer.

Cal-Western Life

The California-Western States Life Insurance Company, better known as Cal-Western Life, provides economic protection and security to individuals, families, and organizations. Licensed in 27 states, it offers all forms of life and health insurance, as well as annuities, pension plans, and equity-based products.

A group of Sacramento Valley business leaders in 1910 started the firm, incorporating as the California State Life Insurance Company. Its first president was Marshall Diggs, hardware merchant and former state senator. The company rented 10 rooms on the fourth floor of a downtown office building and employed three stenographers, a bookkeeper, a "telephone girl," and an errand boy.

In 1912 *The Sacramento Bee* noted that the community's new life insurance company paid its first death claim within 18 hours of the policyholder's demise—initiating a tradition of prompt service to its policyholders and their families which continues to this day. By the close of 1913 insurance in force topped $10 million—a seldom equaled growth record for a company so young.

In 1924, following four years of planning and construction, California State Life moved into its own 14-story building at 10th and J streets. A year later president Diggs died, and J. Roy Kruse succeeded him. The purchase of a small life company in 1928—Inter-Mountain Life of Salt Lake City—helped the Sacramento concern reach its first $100 million of insurance in force.

The firm's name was changed to the present California-Western States Life in 1931, when Cal-State Life acquired Western States Life of San Francisco. The headquarters remained in Sacramento. By 1934 the severity of the Depression was reflected by declining life insurance in force, and Cal-Western Life was racked by dissension and law suits arising out of the recent merger. A new president, O.J. Lacy, infused a new spirit of optimism into the company, and within two years sales regained their momentum.

During World War II 54 Cal-Western Life agents entered the Armed Forces, and production club meetings were canceled for the duration.

Growth resumed after the war, necessitating larger quarters. The company in 1951 broke ground for the new 150,000-square-foot building at 21st and L—a five-story structure, including working basement, which still serves as headquarters today. Cal-Western Life moved into its new quarters over the Thanksgiving weekend in 1952, and two years later, in 1954, achieved its first billion dollars of life insurance in force—the same year that Robert E. Murphy, who came up through the marketing ranks, succeeded O.J. Lacy as president.

The '50s and '60s was a period of remarkable growth for the Sacramento-based concern, an era during which Cal-Western Life became one of the major life insurance carriers domiciled in the West. By the mid-'60s the firm passed the $4-billion mark of life insurance in force—the most basic measurement of life company size—and in late 1966, after securing necessary clearance from the Securities and Exchange Commission, the firm entered the equity field through the introduction of a series of equity-based variable annuity products.

The continued growth and prosperity of this strong, regional insurance carrier attracted the attention in 1967 of the Houston-based American General Insurance Company, a holding company devoted primarily to the life insurance business, which proposed an affiliation with Cal-Western Life through an exchange of stock shares. While the proposal was narrowly defeated by a vote of Cal-Western Life shareowners in 1967, American General continued to build its ownership position in Cal-Western Life during the ensuing years through a series of purchases of Cal-Western stock, including two cash tender offers to the shareowners.

In 1968 Murphy elected to take early retirement and his resignation as president was accepted by the Cal-Western

Life Board, which then installed H Harold Leavey as the corporation's fift president. A 32-year veteran with th company, Leavey was executive vice president at the time of his election an had for many years served as vice-presi dent, general counsel, and secretary.

A new era of leadership wa introduced at Cal-Western Life in 197 with the election of Harold S. Hook, on of the youngest chief executives in th life insurance business. Hook, who wa president of United States Life Insuranc Company, New York City, was th unanimous choice of the board of direc tors following a six-month nationwid search. Leavey, who became chairma until his normal retirement in mid 1971, chaired the selection committe and noted that "Hook's qualities o leadership and previous experienc made him our first choice."

In his nearly five years at the helm o Cal-Western Life, Hook produced dra matic growth for Cal-Western Lif From the close of 1969, the year befor Hook's arrival, to the close of 1975, cor porate earnings increased eightfold t reach $8.2 million, while insurance i force climbed to $8.2 billion and asset to $619.8 million—a record which wor industry-wide attention.

In mid-1975, Hook relinquished th presidency of Cal-Western Life t become president of American Genera Insurance Company (renamed Ameri can General Corporation in 1980) Houston, which by this time was majority owner of Cal-Western Lif shares. He was succeeded by Michael J Poulos, Cal-Western's seventh presi dent, who joined the company in 197(and had been serving as executive vice president.

Later in 1975, through an exchange o stock, American General acquired th balance of Cal-Western Life shares and commencing in 1976, Cal-Wester became a wholly owned subsidiary.

When Poulos resigned the presidency in mid-1978 and moved to Houston t become head of the parent company' life insurance operations, he was suc ceeded by Howard L. Jeske, an attorney

A.

B.

C.

D.

E.

F.

G.

H.

I.

whose service to Cal-Western Life commenced in 1953. At the time of his election, he was senior vice-president/operations and for several years had served as vice-president, general counsel, and secretary. By this time, Cal-Western Life had surpassed $10 billion of life insurance in force and assets were approaching $900 million. Jeske served until 1981, when he was elected chairman and Robert W. Rever became the firm's ninth president. Rever was elected president about a year before Jeske's normal retirement in order to effect an orderly transition of leadership during a period of rapid change in the economic environment.

Presidents of Cal-Western Life
A. Marshall Diggs
    1910
B. J. Roy Kruse
    1925
C. O.J. Lacy
    1934
D. Robert E. Murphy
    1954
E. H. Harold Leavey
    1968
F. Harold S. Hook
    1970
G. Michael J. Poulos
    1975
H. Howard L. Jeske
    1979
I. Robert W. Rever
    1981

Though young in years, the 46-year-old Rever brought 21 years of life insurance experience to the president's office, including 17 with the American General organization, and launched a series of programs to meet the challenges of a then-unfavorable economic environment—including redirection of the marketing thrust, product innovation and development, and improved communications for higher service standards.

Today, under president Rever's stewardship, Cal-Western Life looks forward to an exciting future as a productive member of the nation's most rapidly expanding insurance organization.

Sisters of Mercy

The Sisters of Mercy of Auburn are members of the Roman Catholic order, one of the largest religious congregations in the world, with some 20,000 members around the globe. The Sisters also form the largest religious order serving in the Sacramento diocese, which includes the greater part of Northern California. In Sacramento County they manage three hospital complexes, four elementary schools, and two high schools.

Today the order utilizes sophisticated modern facilities and technologies, but it remains devoted to its original mission of more than 150 years ago: to aid the poor, sick, and uneducated. Through community involvement, the Sisters endeavor to implement the foundress' vision: to connect the rich to the poor, the healthy to the sick, the educated and skilled to the uninstructed, the influential to those of no consequence, the powerful to the weak, to do the work of God on earth.

The order was founded in Dublin, Ireland, by Catherine McAuley on December 12, 1831. A small band of Sisters led by Mother Mary Baptist Russell arrived in San Francisco in 1854. Three years later Mother Mary Baptist and Sister Mary DeSales Reddan took a

The Ridge Home, purchased by the Sisters in 1895, was a private sanitarium located at 22nd and R streets. This home served as the foundation for a new hospital, Mater Misericordiae, commonly known as Sisters Hospital, completed in 1897.

steamer to Sacramento, where Father John Quinn welcomed them at St. Rose's Church, Seventh and K. He showed them an old frame building at the rear of the church, which would be the convent. Undaunted by the primitive facilities, they decided to stay. While the Sisters returned to San Francisco to get ready, the women of Sacramento held a fair to raise funds for the convent and school.

On October 2, 1857, Mother Mary Baptist established the convent behind the church. Three days later five Sisters welcomed 65 students to the school in the church basement. In 1860 the Sisters bought the block bounded by Ninth and Tenth, F and G streets. They used the existing residence for a convent and built a new school. Besides teaching, the Sisters visited the sick and provided

The Sisters of Mercy purchased property bounded by Ninth and Tenth, F and G streets in 1860. The residence served as a convent and school. St. Joseph Academy was incorporated as a high school for girls in 1875.

shelter for the homeless. By 1865 there were 65 orphans in their care. In 1875 the Sisters incorporated the St. Joseph Academy, a high school for girls.

Bishop Patrick Manogue was named to head the diocese of Sacramento, newly independent from San Francisco, in 1886. Mother Mary Vincent Phelan became the first Mother-General in the new diocese, serving from 1887 to 1893 and again from 1896 until her death in 1902.

The Sisters established the Motherhouse at Ninth and G in 1887 and added the Sacred Heart Novitiate to the convent to train young women who wished to be Sisters. On January 4, 1888, four young novices took their vows in a solemn and inspirational ceremony.

The Sisters took over the management of the Stanford Home in 1900, with eight children as their first charges. They ran the home for 36 years, providing shelter for as many as 40 children at one time.

The Sisters kept the school and convent at Ninth and G long after the area changed from residential to commercial, but, keeping up with the city's expansion, they helped to establish schools and medical facilities in the outlying areas. The elementary schools included Sacred Heart, 1934; Our Lady of Fatima, 1947; Holy Spirit, 1950; and St. Robert, 1975. In 1966 the south area gained a new high school named after Bishop Patrick Manogue. The Mercy High School for girls was built in the northeast area on the grounds of Mercy San Juan Hospital.

In 1940 the Motherhouse and Novitiate were moved to Auburn, in the foothills about 30 miles north of Sacramento. The Convent of Our Lady of Mercy is the center of the Mercy Community, providing guidance, training,

To meet the needs of Sacramento's neighboring city, Folsom, Mercy Hospital of Folsom was acquired on July 1, 1980, by the Sisters of Mercy.

and spiritual renewal. It is also the home of the General Council of the Sisters of Mercy. Its beautiful facilities are used as a retreat center by religious women from around the world.

Mercy Health Care Organization

The Sisters have provided health care for the people of Sacramento County since their arrival in 1857, and hospital care since 1895. Through the corporate umbrella, the Mercy Health Care Organization, they now manage and staff three hospital complexes in Sacramento County and one in Redding.

The Sisters' mission statement declares their commitment to the healing arts: "We acknowledge health as a basic human value and commit our efforts to promote, preserve, protect, and restore wellness whenever we are able. We acknowledge sickness, suffering, and death as integral aspects of human life and as occasions when God can be experienced. In these moments we strive to offer hope, healing, and peace."

During their first three decades in Sacramento, the Sisters visited the sick in their homes, often walking through muddy or dusty streets with food and medicines to alleviate distress. In 1895 the Sisters purchased the Ridge Home, a private sanitarium, at 22nd and R. The

next year they broke ground for a larger facility on the next block, 23rd and R. This hospital was completed in 1897. Named the Mater Misericordiae, it was more commonly known as Sisters Hospital.

In the same year the Sisters opened the Mater Misericordiae Training School of Nurses. The hospital expanded in the next few years, adding a well-equipped operating room in 1900, a beautiful little chapel in 1905, a new wing and additional surgical facilities in 1908, a 17-bed ward for men in 1914, and an annex for additional patients in 1918. By the 1920s the hospital could care for 100 patients and was still growing.

In 1923 the Sisters bought a seven-acre site bounded by 40th, H, I, and J streets for a new, four-story hospital, which was completed two years later. It

had a capacity of 155 beds plus 35 bassinets. At its dedication in 1925, Mayor Albert Elkus expressed Sacramento's pride in the new facility: "Its magnificence of structure, its capable and efficient staff, and its modern equipment give Sacramento the added prestige that good hospitals give to any community."

In 1944 the Sisters, with the help of the people of Redding, purchased the 45-bed St. Caroline Hospital in that city and took over its management. Early in 1947 they bought the present Clairmont Heights site, 11 acres overlooking Redding, with a view of Mt. Shasta. The new Mercy Hospital of Redding was dedicated in 1953, and has been expanded several times since.

As the population of Sacramento grew rapidly during the postwar years, the need for health services increased. In 1950 the two-story Mercy Children's Hospital was opened at 3994 H Street, behind the main hospital. Friends of the Sisters organized the Mercy Hospital Foundation to raise and manage funds for expansion.

In 1954 the East Wing addition to the main hospital was completed, bringing the total number of beds to 250 plus 60

Sister Mary Peter, while serving her 29-year tenure, was an inspiration to patients, their families, and employees. Under her direction, a children's clinic was opened for underprivileged children, the Children's Hospital built, the east wing and extended care facility added, and the Mercy Guild founded.

bassinets. The following year the Marsh Memorial physical therapy unit was built next to Children's Hospital, featuring a full-size therapeutic swimming pool. In 1959 the intensive care unit opened, the only one of its kind in the greater Sacramento area. In 1963 the 50-bed Mercy Convalescent Unit—later named Mercy Extended Care Facility—was opened to provide extended care through skilled nursing services.

Responding to the health needs of the rapidly growing number of north area families, the Sisters on February 15, 1967, opened Mercy San Juan Hospital, a 211-bed acute care facility offering a full range of medical and surgical services. Besides the most modern of equipment for diagnosis and treatment, Mercy San Juan offers complete, personalized health care and follow-up services. It sponsors community health educational programs.

The Mercy Hospital of Sacramento at

On October 2, 1982, the Sisters of Mercy of Auburn celebrated their 125th anniversary of serving the health care, education, and spiritual needs of the greater Sacramento communities. Like the foundress, Mother McAuley (shown here), the Sisters of Mercy continue their dedicated mission. (Photo courtesy of Kurt Fishback.)

40th and J expanded its facilities again in 1981, with the dedication of the Sister Mary Peter Pavilion. On July 1, 1980, the Sisters acquired a 34-bed hospital in the town of Folsom. Shortly afterwards they began extensive remodeling of the emergency room and the adjacent radiology department. Long-range plans include continual improvement and expansion.

On March 1, 1981, the Mercy Health Care Organization (MHCO) was created to provide guidance for the continuing growth of Mercy services. Sister Eileen Barrett, with many years of experience in nursing and hospital administration, was appointed chief executive officer. Besides the president, the MHCO staff includes the vice-president of operations, director of finance, director of management information services, director of human resources, and director of mission services.

Sister Kathleen Dunne, former Superior General, launched the comprehensive study of the system which resulted in the formation of MHCO. "The MHCO gives us a way to work together with the local communities we serve in developing policies for all the hospitals. It enables us to make long-

Responding to the health care needs of a growing Sacramento community, the Sisters of Mercy opened Mercy San Juan Hospital on February 15, 1967.

term as well as immediate decisions," she explained.

Sister Maura Power became Superior General in 1982, with responsibility for all of the Mercy programs—in health care, education, and social work.

The Mercy health care system in the greater Sacramento area includes hundreds of employees and many dedicated physicians who care for thousands of patients each year. The Sisters have proven incredibly successful in mobilizing resources to meet the physical, emotional, and spiritual needs of Sacramento Valley residents.

Mercy Hospital Volunteers

Volunteers from all walks of life help the Sisters of Mercy in their mission to provide health care. In 1981 more than 2,100 volunteers donated over 110,000 service hours to the three hospitals in the area—Sacramento, San Juan, and Folsom.

Traditionally, volunteers have played a vital role in administration and policy making, fund raising, and patient care. The human and spiritual benefit—to volunteers and patients alike—is beyond reckoning.

At the policy-making level, community leaders serve on the board of

trustees of the Mercy Health Care Organization. Physicians donate their time to serve on medical committees. Leaders and professionals serve on the 48-member Mercy Foundation board of governors, whose responsibility is to pursue, invest, and distribute philanthropic dollars to the Sacramento and San Juan hospitals.

Fund-raising activities involve special events, estate planning, direct mail and foundation and corporate giving. Individuals, families, and businesses have responded generously to requests for funds, enabling the Sisters to offer area residents the most modern, up-to-date equipment and medical facilities.

Mercy guilds and auxiliaries assist in both fund raising and patient care. Sacramento and San Juan have guilds; Folsom has an auxiliary. They organize special events such as jog-a-thons, hole-in-one golf tournaments, sporting contests, and social gatherings. They sew and sell decorative items in the hospital gift shops. Guild units are located as far away as Yuba City and Marysville, where a group of about 40 members meets regularly to create gift items for the support of the Mercy Children's Hospital in Sacramento.

The various guilds grew out of the Children's Hospital Guild, which was

The Sister Mary Peter Pavilion

Mercy Hospital of Sacramento, formerly Mercy General Hospital, as it looks today.

Patients, families, and hospital staff all benefit from the emotional and spiritual support provided by the Sisters and employees who work in pastoral care services. This important service is a tradition in all Mercy health care facilities. (Photo courtesy of Kurt Fishback.)

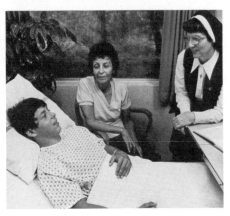

founded in 1953 when the old Mercy Nursing School at 3994 H was converted into a pediatrics unit. Guild members wore pink uniforms; the young patients called them the Pink Ladies. Junior Guild members—young women from ages 12 to 18—wore pink-and-white striped uniforms and were called the Peppermints.

Through the years hospital volunteers have been involved in patient care. They staff the information desk, escort patients to their rooms, wheel the gift cart to patients' bedsides, and provide reassurance and a helping hand wherever needed. They also staff blood banks, assist in laboratories, and sew stuffed puppies and bears to give to children in the hospital. On Thanksgiving, Christmas, Halloween, and other special occasions, volunteers often make gifts and decorations to add a festive air.

Of the newer programs are the Hospice Programs of Mercy Sacramento and San Juan hospitals, in which trained volunteers work closely with the hospital staff to help patients and families faced with a terminal illness. In the hospital or at home, the hospice team provides nursing care, companionship, and spiritual comfort in coping with the many dimensions of dying with peace and dignity.

As medical science changes, the roles of volunteers also evolve. Yet no matter how complex technology becomes, the need for human contact and human caring seems to be an essential part of health and well-being. Mercy volunteers have contributed greatly to the quality of health care in the Mercy hospitals.

California State University, Sacramento

Sacramentans worked together with the state of California to establish the Capital Campus of the State University system; and in return, the university and its alumni have contributed valuable resources, skills, and knowledge to the community. "Public higher education has played a vital part in the development of the dynamic economy and cultural ambience which continues to make Sacramento an ideal place to work and live," president W. Lloyd Johns recently observed.

Located amid rolling lawns and groves of trees by the historic American River, the California State University, Sacramento, offers bachelor's and master's degrees in over 50 academic specialties. Its six-story library offers information on almost every conceivable subject. Its music, drama, guest speakers, seminars, and educational programs attract audiences from all walks of life.

Obtaining state approval for the capital city location took 16 years. That perseverance paid off in 1947, when Senator Earl D. Desmond of Sacramento successfully steered the funding bill through the state legislature. The board of trustees appointed Dr. Guy Ashley West from Chico State College to serve

Surrounded by books, a student concentrates on her assignment.

Dr. Guy Ashley West, first president of CSUS, led the university's development for 18 years.

Dr. W. Lloyd Johns has headed the Capital Campus since 1978.

as founding president, a position he held for the next 18 years. For its first five years the new college shared the classrooms and campus facilities of Sacramento Junior College (now Sacramento City College) on Freeport Boulevard.

When the 1949 legislature authorized funds to construct a separate campus, trustees selected a 300-acre peach orchard along the scenic American

River on the eastern edge of the city. The cornerstone for the new Administration Building was laid on October 25, 1952, and within a few months the fledgling campus boasted a library, one large classroom facility (Douglass Hall), three science units, a cafeteria, and 13 temporary structures.

The college moved into its permanent home early in 1953. That fall more than 2,700 students registered for classes. Upon completion of the University Theatre, the college inaugurated a tradition of high-quality theatrical productions. By 1959 it had added a third floor to the library and new wings to the Administration Building and the cafeteria. Three residence halls provided on-campus housing for students.

As campus facilities expanded, so did academic offerings. When the State Education Code was modified in 1959 to permit colleges as well as universities to offer advanced degrees in liberal arts, Sacramento added master's programs in English, art, history, economics, life science, mathematics, music, and psychology, and expanded its engineering programs.

The California State Colleges were unified into one statewide system of 19 campuses in 1961—the largest system of four-year public higher education in the world. In 1972 the system was designated State Universities and Colleges, and the Capital City campus became California State University, Sacramento, abbreviated CSUS, but informally still known nostalgically as "Sac State."

Two campus landmarks are particularly symbolic of the interrelationship between the community and the university. The new University Library, constructed in 1974, dominates the central skyline as the tallest building on campus. With a capacity of more than 740,000 volumes, it is used by alumni

political leaders often give guest lectures on campus.

Many of the university's research and training programs reinforce the Valley's attractiveness to business and industry. The School of Engineering and Computer Science, which has developed a unique biomedical engineering program, is noted for its expertise in computer-assisted design and manufacturing. While training future leaders, the School of Business and Public Administration provides on-going assistance to the business community through conference, technical assistance, and maintenance of a comprehensive data base

television with two-way audio systems, so that they may communicate directly with the on-campus instructor.

Two nonprofit foundations, both created in 1951, help support the university's programs. Representatives from the community and the campus share policy-making responsibilities on the boards of directors. The Foundation of CSUS assists faculty members and others associated with the university to obtain funding for special projects. It also administers endowments, scholarships, loans, and various other accounts. The Hornet Foundation oversees food services, bookstores, and vending

and community members as well as faculty and students.

The Guy West Bridge, completed in 1967, is a graceful twin-tower suspension span that resembles a miniature Golden Gate as it links the university to a burgeoning complex of commercial offices and condominiums across the American River. The bridge was built by private enterprise, presented to the city, and named in honor of the university's first president.

As the Capital Campus, CSUS hosts a systemwide internship program which provides students with practical experience in government. Reciprocally,

The six-story University Library, built in 1974, serves campus and community with its vast collection of books, journals, government documents, videotapes, and microfilm spanning the spectrum of human knowledge.

---

on local economic conditions.

Recently CSUS has embarked on an ambitious program to make educational services more accessible throughout its 13-county service area through telecommunications technology. From their homes or neighborhood centers, students will be able to take courses by

enterprises, many of which are located in the University Union, completed in 1974.

By 1982 CSUS had over 2,000 employees, including faculty, staff, and administrative personnel. Enrollment for the 1981-1982 school year exceeded 22,000 students, from throughout California and the nation and from more than 90 foreign nations.

The current president, W. Lloyd Johns, who came to the campus in 1978, stated: "A society that encourages public higher education reaps tangible and spiritual rewards worth many times its original investment."

PATRONS

The following individuals, companies, and organizations have made a valuable commitment to the quality of this publication. Windsor Publications and the Sacramento County Historical Society gratefully acknowledge their participation in *Sacramento: Heart of the Golden State.*

The Acorn
  Sue T. Noack, Owner
Aerojet-General Corporation*
Arden Fair Shopping Center
Bank of America NT & SA,
  Sacramento Headquarters
BARRATT SACRAMENTO
Bel Air Markets*
M.J. Brock & Sons, Inc.
  (Larchmont Homes)*
California Almond Growers
  Exchange*
California State University,
  Sacramento*
Cal-Western Life*
Illa Collin, Sacramento County
  Supervisor, District 2
Crystal Cream and Butter
  Company*
Days Inns of America, Inc.
Diepenbrock, Wulff, Plant &
  Hannegan*
Emigh Hardware Store*
Mr. & Mrs. Stanley C. Engs
Dr. & Mrs. D. Jackson
  Faustman
Federal Express Corporation

The Firehouse Restaurant
FIRST Federal Credit Union
Gerlinger Motor Parts, Inc.*
Bill and Naida Geyer
Golden State Business Systems
Douglas W. Griffith
Mr. & Mrs. Archie Hefner
Hiroshima, Jacobs and Roth
Hobrecht's Lighting*
The Lock Agency
McGeorge School of Law/
  University of the Pacific*
"Macy's Sacramento Charter
  Members"
Main Hurdman
Mansion Inn
Sandra K. & Frank E. Marcello
Martyr & Curry*
National Organization for
  Women, Sacramento Area
  Chapter
Noack and Dean
North Sacramento Land
  Company*
The Palm Iron and Bridge
  Works*
Price Waterhouse

RJB Company*
Marjorie J. Reid
River City Office Supply
The Sacramento Bee*
Sacramento History Center
Sacramento Pioneer
  Association
The Sacramento Union*
Simms Hardware Company,
  Inc.*
Sisters of Mercy*
A. Teichert & Son, Inc.*
The Thomson-Diggs
  Company*
Weinstock's Department Store*
WEMCO*
Wind Gap Gallery of Fine Art*
  Leafy Mayhew, Owner/
  Director

*Partners in Progress of
Sacramento: Heart of the Golden State. The histories of these companies and organizations appear in Chapter 8, beginning on page 121.

SUGGESTED READING

Sacramento is extremely fortunate in having two daily newspapers dating back to the 1850s: the *Sacramento Bee* and the *Sacramento Union*. These have provided a diary of events continuously for nearly as long as the city has been in existence, and have been the primary source of material included in this book.

The most comprehensive historical work on the city and county was done in 1880 by two researchers, Thomas Thompson and Albert West. Their book, *Illustrated History of Sacramento County*, was republished by Howell-North, San Francisco, 1959. In addition to giving information on the Sutter years, fires and floods, churches, schools, voluntary associations, transportation, and many more topics, it contains detailed line drawings of numerous homes, offices, and street scenes.

Four successive county histories relied mainly on Thompson and West for historical data. In addition, they each contain biographical information about many Sacramento citizens and their families. They are as follows:

Davis, Winfield J. *An Illustrated History of Sacramento County, California*. Chicago: The Lewis Publishing Co., 1890.

Reed, G. Walter, ed. *History of Sacramento County, California*. Los Angeles: Historic Record Company, 1923.

Willis, William L. *History of Sacramento County, California*. Los Angeles: Historic Record Company, 1913.

Wooldridge, Major J. W., ed. *History of the Sacramento Valley, California*. Chicago: Pioneer Historical Publishing Co., 1931.

Coinciding nicely with the development of Old Sacramento as a tourist attraction, a number of recent works have focused on the early days. Among them are the following:

Neasham, V. Aubrey, James E. Henley, and Janice A. Woodruff. *The City of the Plain: Sacramento in the Nineteenth Century*. Sacramento: The Sacramento Pioneer Foundation, 1969.

Mims, Julie and Kevin. *Sacramento: A Pictorial History of California's Capital*. Sacramento: Sacramento Savings & Loan Association, 1981.

Severson, Thor. *Sacramento: An Illustrated History: 1839 to 1874*. Sacramento: California Historical Society, 1973.

Smith, Jesse, ed. *Sketches of Old Sacramento*. Sacramento: Sacramento County Historical Society, 1976.

Numerous books and articles have been written about some of the most romantic episodes prior to 1880; in particular, the Sutter years, the Gold Rush, and the building of the transcontinental railroad. For starters, we would recommend the following to the modern reader:

Dillon, Richard. *Fool's Gold: A Biography of John Sutter*. New York: Coward-McCann, Inc., 1967.

Holliday, J.S. *The World Rushed In: The California Gold Rush Experience*. New York: Simon and Schuster, 1981.

Kraus, George. *High Road to Promontory*. Palo Alto: American West Publishing Co., 1969.

In addition the Sacramento County Historical Society has published an extensive collection of booklets, the *Golden Notes,* on various aspects of the county's history from the early days to more recent times.

Sources on the Twentieth Century

The present work is unique in its attempt to trace the development of metropolitan Sacramento since the Thompson and West county history came out in 1880. Although newspaper and magazine articles abound, this is the first book telling the story of modern times in the capital city of California.

One other book came close. Some twenty years ago the senior author of the present work, Dr. Joseph A. McGowan, compiled a broad overview, *History of the Sacramento Valley* (New York: Lewis Historical Publishing Co., 1961). This work included cities and counties in the northern part of the valley as well as Sacramento. It is particularly valuable for its perspective on the interrelationship between valley cities, the changing economy, and the impact of transportation and agriculture.

For the city's development since 1880 we relied on a variety of sources, but primarily on the *Bee* and *Union*. We supplemented newspaper sources by going to city and county records and using the resources of the Sacramento Housing and Redevelopment Agency and the Sacramento Metropolitan Chamber of Commerce.

Recently the Sacramento History Center has become the chief repository for information about the city and county. When the new building is completed in Old Sacramento, it will be readily accessible to the public. For those interested in delving further into any of the topics covered in this book, a list of specific references will be on file with the History Center.

INDEX

Italicized numbers indicate illustrations.

Automobile travel caused the advent of a new sight on the American landscape—the corner gas station. This Standard Oil station was associated with the Sacramento Tire Company at 1530 L Street during the 1930s and 1940s. Courtesy, Sacramento City-County Library Collection, Sacramento Museum and History Division

CALIFORNIA
STEAM NAVIGATION
COMPANY.

Organized March 1st, 1854. - - - **Capital Stock, $2,500,000.**

The following are the Officers for the Years 1869-70.

President, B. M. HARTSHORNE ; Vice President, W. H. TAYLOR ; Secretary, S. O. PUTNAM ; Trustees, B. M. HARTSHORNE, W. H. TAYLOR, A. HAYWARD, W. C. RALSTON, WM. ALVORD, A. REDINGTON, LLOYD TEVIS, JOHN BENSLEY and S. F. BUTTERWORTH. Agents —Sacramento, ALFRED REDINGTON ; Marysville, C. H. KIMBALL ; Red Bluff, SAMUEL JAYNES ; Stockton, T. C. WALKER.

Departure from Broadway Wharf,
CARRYING THE UNITED STATES MAILS.

Steamer CAPITAL	Capt. E. A. POOLE.
Steamer YOSEMITE	Capt. E. A. POOLE.
Steamer CHRYSOPOLIS	Capt. A. FOSTER.
Steamer ANTELOPE	Capt. CHARLES THORNE.
Steamer JULIA	Capt. W. BROMLEY.
Steamer AMADOR	Capt. JOHN FOURATT.

ONE OF THE ABOVE STEAMERS WILL

Leave every day, at four o'clock, P.M.
(SUNDAYS EXCEPTED) FOR

SACRAMENTO and STOCKTON,

Connecting with the Light-Draught Steamers for

MARYSVILLE, COLUSA AND RED BLUFF.

For further particulars, apply at the OFFICE OF THE COMPANY,

N.E. Cor. Jackson and Front Sts., San Francisco.
B. M. HARTSHORNE, President.

The California Steam Navigation Company, which ran steamers from San Francisco to Red Bluff, was eventually bought out by the Central Pacific Railroad Company which then controlled both river and rail service in Sacramento. This advertisement dates from 1869. Courtesy, Norman L. Wilson